The Probabilistic Mindset

Mastering Uncertainty to Make Smarter Decisions in Life and Work

Deepanshu Suman

First Edition 2025

Clarity, Resilience, and Strategy in an Uncertain World

Copyright

Title: The Probabilistic Mindset
Author: Deepanshu Suman

First Edition
ISBN: 978-93-344-5899-2

Disclaimer: This book is for informational and educational purposes only. It explores concepts of probability, decision-making, and strategic thinking. Nothing in this book should be interpreted as financial, investment, legal, or professional advice. Readers are encouraged to seek independent guidance before acting on any ideas discussed herein.

Dedication

To those who choose clarity over comfort,
and curiosity over certainty.
To the thinkers who question patterns,
the builders who embrace randomness,
and the dreamers who keep playing long games
in a short-sighted world.
May your decisions be wise,
your risks be measured,
and your mind forever probabilistic.

Acknowledgments

Writing a book about uncertainty is, in itself, an act of uncertainty. This project would not have reached completion without the many people who added clarity, encouragement, and perspective along the way.

To my family for grounding me when ideas drifted too far into abstraction, and for reminding me that wisdom is only meaningful when it improves real life.

To my friends and collaborators the thinkers, readers, and quiet contrarians who challenged assumptions, asked better questions, and helped refine messy thoughts into coherent frameworks.

To the countless authors, economists, investors, and philosophers whose work shaped my understanding of probability, risk, and human behavior this book stands on your intellectual shoulders.

To the readers who see the world not as fixed, but as fluid and full of possibilities you are the reason this book exists. May it help you navigate the unknown with greater calm, curiosity, and courage.

Deepanshu Suman

Preface Why I Wrote This Book

Most people make decisions as if the world were predictable as if effort always led to results, intelligence guaranteed success, and the future could be reasoned into obedience. But life rarely plays by such clean rules. The world is messy, dynamic, and full of randomness. Even the best plans collide with chance.

I wrote this book because I wanted to understand and teach how to think clearly when outcomes are uncertain. The first time I realized how little control we actually have, it wasn't comforting. It was humbling. Yet, paradoxically, learning to see life probabilistically didn't make me more anxious it made me freer. When you stop expecting certainty, you start designing for resilience. You stop chasing perfect answers and begin optimizing for better odds.

The *probabilistic mindset* is not about gambling or statistics. It's a philosophy of decision-making a way of navigating reality that combines rationality with humility. It asks a simple but transformative question: *"Given what I know now, what's the smartest bet I can make?"*

This book is my attempt to map that mindset to build a bridge between probability theory and everyday life. It draws from psychology, investing, systems thinking, and philosophy. You'll find practical frameworks for making better decisions, stories of people who thrived under uncertainty, and mental models for separating luck from skill.

I don't claim to have mastered uncertainty no one has. But I've learned that mastery isn't about control; it's about calibration. It's about learning to update your beliefs, adapt your strategy, and stay calm when the dice roll against you. That's what this book aims to teach: not how to predict the future, but how to thrive in spite of it.

If you finish this book thinking a little more probabilistically, judging yourself a little less harshly for randomness, and making decisions with a little more clarity it will have served its purpose.

Deepanshu Suman

How to Use This Book

This book is not meant to be read like a textbook it's meant to be *used* like a mental operating system. You can read it linearly from start to finish, or dip into specific parts depending on where you are in your decision-making journey. Either way, the goal is the same: to train your mind to think in probabilities, not certainties.

Each part builds on the last:

- **Part I Foundations of Probability Thinking** Explores how uncertainty works, why humans struggle with it, and the mental errors that cloud judgment.
- **Part II Building the Probabilistic Mindset** Translates theory into practical tools: scenario planning, Bayesian updating, decision templates, and emotional detachment.
- **Part III Applications of the Probabilistic Mindset** Applies these ideas to real domains investing, entrepreneurship, personal choices, creativity, and negotiation.
- **Part IV Mastery & Long-Term Perspective** Focuses on resilience, optionality, compounding mental edges, and the philosophy of living well with uncertainty.

Within chapters, you'll find:

- **Concept sections** that explain key ideas clearly and concisely.
- **Models and frameworks** you can apply directly to real-world decisions.
- **Reflections and exercises** designed to shift how you perceive randomness and control.

Think of this book as a toolkit. Don't rush it. The ideas will make the most sense when you *pause* to consider how they apply to your own life. Highlight generously. Write in the margins. Question the assumptions even mine. That's how probabilistic thinkers grow sharper.

Finally, remember: this book won't make uncertainty disappear. Nothing will. What it can do is give you a framework a lens to see risk, luck, and randomness more clearly. When you start seeing life probabilistically, you stop fearing uncertainty and start using it.

Deepanshu Suman

Glossary of Key Terms

Probability A measure of uncertainty not about what *will* happen, but about how confident we can be in what *might* happen. In this book, probability is used not as mere mathematics, but as a lens for reasoning, decision-making, and understanding the world.

Probabilistic Thinking The discipline of viewing reality through likelihoods instead of absolutes. It replaces "yes/no" thinking with "how likely" thinking sharpening judgment, reducing overconfidence, and enabling rational action under uncertainty.

Expected Value (EV) A decision model that weighs potential outcomes by their probability and impact:

$$EV = (\text{Probability of Outcome}) \times (\text{Impact of Outcome})$$

High-quality decisions tend to have positive expected value even if individual outcomes sometimes fail.

Bayesian Updating The continuous refinement of beliefs as new evidence emerges. You begin with a prior belief, gather new data, and update your confidence accordingly mirroring how the human brain naturally learns and adapts.

Decision Quality A measure of how sound a decision is at the moment it is made, based on information, probabilities, and reasoning not its eventual result. A good decision can have a poor outcome if randomness intervenes, and vice versa.

Noise Random variability that clouds judgment or distorts signals in data. Mastery lies in distinguishing the *signal* (useful information) from *noise* (random fluctuation).

Black Swan Event A rare, unpredictable event with massive impact whether catastrophic (a financial crisis) or transformative (a scientific breakthrough). While such events cannot be predicted precisely, you can design systems that are robust or even benefit from their occurrence.

Second-Order Thinking The ability to think beyond immediate effects by asking, "And then what?" It examines the ripple effects of decisions across time, systems, and feedback loops, rather than focusing on first-order consequences.

Asymmetric Risk A situation in which potential upside vastly outweighs potential downside (or vice versa). Great investors, entrepreneurs, and thinkers seek positive asymmetry big potential gains with limited possible loss.

Compounding The exponential growth that results when small advantages are applied consistently over time. Probabilistic thinkers compound not only wealth but also knowledge, habits, and judgment.

Cognitive Bias A systematic error in perception, reasoning, or judgment that distorts how we interpret probability, risk, and causality. Examples include confirmation bias, hindsight bias, and overconfidence bias.

Mental Model A conceptual framework that simplifies complex reality and aids decision-making. Mental models are cognitive shortcuts that, when combined, form a powerful toolkit for navigating uncertainty. Probabilistic thinking is itself a meta-model integrating many others.

Calibration The alignment between your confidence and your actual accuracy. If you claim to be "70% sure" and are correct about 70% of the time, you are well-calibrated a hallmark of expert judgment.

Optionality The capacity to act on opportunities as they emerge. Maintaining optionality means preserving flexibility and adaptability creating a system that can pivot toward upside and limit exposure to downside.

Fat Tail A statistical term describing extreme, rare events that occur more frequently than traditional (normal) models predict. Real-world systems markets, societies, and ecosystems are often fat-tailed, meaning improbable events happen more often than intuition suggests.

Regret Minimization A forward-looking strategy that asks: "Which decision will I regret less in the long run?" It shifts focus from short-term comfort to enduring satisfaction and long-term alignment.

Rationality Not the absence of emotion, but disciplined alignment between beliefs, evidence, and goals. True rationality integrates emotion as feedback anchoring clarity of thought with purposeful action.

Uncertainty vs. Risk Risk refers to situations where probabilities are known.

Uncertainty describes scenarios where probabilities are unknown or unknowable.

Most of life falls into the latter and probabilistic thinking equips you to operate effectively within it.

Feedback Loop A cyclical process in which actions generate outcomes that inform future actions. Strong feedback loops accelerate learning, calibration, and performance improvement over time.

Robustness The ability of a person, system, or idea to endure shocks without breaking. Robustness thrives not on perfect prediction, but on flexibility, adaptability, and preparation for the unexpected.

Introduction

What Is a Probabilistic Mindset?

Most people approach life as if it is predictable, as if the future is a straight line from cause to effect. We treat decisions as binary, outcomes as guaranteed, and our own knowledge as sufficient to anticipate what comes next. But reality is rarely so neat.

A *probabilistic mindset* is the habit of thinking in terms of likelihoods rather than absolutes. It is the mental framework that asks:

> *"Given what I know now, what are the possible outcomes, and how likely are they?"*

This mindset doesn't aim to eliminate uncertainty. Instead, it teaches you to navigate it intelligently. Probabilistic thinking allows you to make better decisions under imperfect information, manage risk without fear, and recognize where luck, skill, and chance intersect. It turns randomness from an enemy into a tool.

In essence, the probabilistic mindset is about replacing black-and-white thinking with shades of probability. It's a lens through which every decision from career choices to investments, relationships to health can be evaluated more accurately and realistically.

Why Deterministic Thinking Fails

Deterministic thinking assumes that outcomes follow predictable rules. If you perform action A, then result B is guaranteed. This approach is comforting because it simplifies the world, but it is often dangerously misleading.

Consider investing, entrepreneurship, or even personal decisions: no matter how careful or skilled you are, outcomes are influenced by countless variables beyond your control. Deterministic thinking blinds you to the role of randomness, making you overconfident and underprepared for rare but impactful events.

Research in behavioral economics and cognitive psychology shows that humans naturally overestimate their predictive power. We see patterns where none exist, overvalue recent trends, and underestimate extreme events. Deterministic thinking is a trap; it convinces us we understand the future better than we actually do.

A probabilistic mindset corrects for this bias. By evaluating likelihoods instead of certainties, you accept the limits of your knowledge and design decisions that are robust to a range of outcomes not just the one you hope for.

The Illusion of Certainty

Certainty is seductive. We crave it because it reduces anxiety and makes planning feel safe. Yet most forms of "certainty" in life are illusions. Even scientific predictions, financial forecasts, or strategic plans operate under assumptions that can be wrong.

The illusion of certainty can manifest in many ways:

- Believing that past patterns guarantee future results.
- Treating anecdotal evidence as universally applicable.
- Ignoring rare, high-impact events because they seem improbable.

The danger is not that we are wrong, but that we are *confidently wrong*. This is where probabilistic thinking becomes essential: it teaches humility without paralysis. By acknowledging uncertainty, you can weigh risks, anticipate variability, and act decisively even when the future is unclear.

How Probability Shapes Every Choice

Probability is not an abstract mathematical concept reserved for statisticians. It underpins virtually every decision we make from choosing a career path, negotiating a contract, or deciding whether to take a trip, to managing your finances, health, and relationships.

For example:

- **Career Decisions:** Choosing a role or project is rarely a guaranteed path to success. Instead, each option has probabilities of skill development, network expansion, financial gain, and personal satisfaction.
- **Investing:** Every investment carries expected value. Some choices may have small chances of massive payoffs, others high likelihood of mediocre returns. Evaluating probabilities allows you to allocate capital intelligently.

- **Relationships:** Social networks, friendships, and partnerships operate like compounding systems. Probabilistic thinking helps assess trust, compatibility, and long-term potential without being swayed by immediate emotions.

Every choice is a bet consciously or unconsciously on future outcomes. Probabilistic thinking allows you to make these bets with clarity, to quantify risk versus reward, and to understand how small advantages accumulate over time. It is a framework for life, turning uncertainty from a source of fear into a source of opportunity.

In the chapters that follow, we will explore the foundations, tools, and applications of probabilistic thinking. You will learn to recognize biases, evaluate risk, and structure decisions that are resilient to randomness. By the end of this book, you will see that uncertainty is not a problem to be solved, but a reality to be mastered.

Contents

Part I

Foundations of Probability Thinking

Chapter 1

The Nature of Uncertainty

Imagine standing at the edge of a cliff, peering into a dense fog that stretches as far as the eye can see. You know the ground is there somewhere, but you cannot see it. Every step forward carries risk a slip could be harmless, or it could be fatal. Yet you must move. This is the essence of uncertainty: the invisible forces that shape outcomes beyond our immediate perception, the hidden probabilities that determine success or failure, and the unknowable events that can upend even the most carefully laid plans.

Life is full of these "foggy cliffs." From the stock market and business ventures to personal relationships and health decisions, the future is rarely predictable. What we often call luck, chance, or fate is merely the manifestation of complex systems interacting in ways we cannot fully control. And yet, humans have an innate desire to impose order, to find patterns, and to believe that the world can be tamed into deterministic rules.

In this chapter, we will explore the very nature of uncertainty the chaos and randomness inherent in life, the mental frameworks humans use to interpret it, and the psychological resistance we have to accepting that not everything can be predicted. By understanding these forces, you will begin to see why probabilistic thinking is not just a tool, but a necessity for navigating a world where certainty is the exception, not the rule.

1.1 Chaos, Randomness, and Unpredictability

At first glance, chaos and randomness may seem like synonyms, but they describe distinct aspects of uncertainty. Understanding the difference is essential for developing a probabilistic mindset, because it allows you to identify what can be modeled, what can only be prepared for, and what is fundamentally unknowable.

Chaos: Deterministic but Unpredictable

Chaos refers to systems that are governed by deterministic rules meaning they follow precise mathematical or physical laws but whose outcomes are extremely sensitive to initial conditions. This phenomenon is often called the "butterfly effect": the idea that a butterfly flapping its wings in Brazil could, theoretically, set off a chain of events that alters weather patterns in North America.

Even though chaotic systems are deterministic in principle, predicting their long-term behavior is practically impossible. Small variations in starting conditions amplify over time, making precise forecasts unreliable. Examples include:

- Weather systems: Meteorologists can forecast a few days ahead with reasonable accuracy, but long-term predictions remain uncertain.
- Planetary orbits and celestial mechanics: Tiny gravitational variations can make some orbital paths unpredictable over millions of years.
- Human behavior in large systems: While individual actions may follow patterns, the combined behavior of millions of people can produce chaotic outcomes.

The key takeaway is that chaos does not mean "lawless" it means that complexity and sensitivity limit our ability to forecast outcomes with certainty. Probabilistic thinking embraces this limitation by focusing on likely ranges, distributions, and contingencies rather than precise predictions.

Randomness: Inherent Uncertainty

Randomness, by contrast, is genuinely unpredictable. It refers to events or outcomes that occur without deterministic cause or pattern where probability is the only reliable framework for understanding potential results. Randomness can appear in nature, human systems, and even in engineered processes. Examples include:

- Rolling dice or drawing cards: Each outcome is independent and equally probable.
- Stock market fluctuations in the short term: Noise and sentiment create variability that is fundamentally uncertain.
- Genetic mutations: Random changes in DNA introduce variability in evolution.

Random events are irreducible no amount of analysis can precisely predict them. But they can be quantified probabilistically. For instance, while you cannot predict the exact roll of a die, you can assign a $1/6$ chance to each outcome and make decisions accordingly. Understanding randomness allows you to structure decisions around probabilities, expected values, and risk management.

Unpredictability: The Intersection of Chaos and Randomness

Unpredictability arises when chaos and randomness combine. In many real-world systems from financial markets to ecosystems to global politics both deterministic sensitivity and inherent randomness coexist. This makes long-term outcomes extremely difficult to foresee. Examples include:

- Stock market crashes: Influenced by investor behavior (chaotic) and unforeseen events like natural disasters or regulatory changes (random).
- Pandemic spread: Biological dynamics are governed by deterministic viral properties, but human interactions and mutations introduce randomness.
- Technological adoption: Predictable trends exist, yet sudden cultural shifts or breakthroughs create unexpected results.

The practical lesson is that unpredictability is the default state of complex systems. Attempting to treat these systems as deterministic leads to overconfidence, poor planning, and avoidable risk. Probabilistic thinking teaches us to work with distributions, stress-test scenarios, and consider a wide range of plausible outcomes rather than relying on a single forecast.

Applying These Insights

Recognizing chaos, randomness, and unpredictability changes how you approach decisions:

- Focus on **robust strategies** that perform reasonably well under many possible futures, rather than betting everything on a single predicted outcome.
- Use **ranges and probabilities** instead of point predictions embrace uncertainty as a measure of information, not a source of fear.
- Identify where **predictive models are useful** (low chaos, low randomness) and where they are misleading (high chaos, high randomness).
- Treat rare, high-impact events as important even if unlikely "black swans" are the inevitable result of complex, unpredictable systems.

In the next sections, we will explore frameworks that help distinguish between what can be known, what can be estimated probabilistically, and what remains fundamentally uncertain. By understanding the nature of chaos, randomness, and unpredictability, you begin to see why embracing a probabilistic mindset is not optional it is essential for navigating reality effectively.

1.2 Known Knowns, Known Unknowns, and Unknown Unknowns

One of the most powerful ways to understand uncertainty is through the framework introduced by former U.S. Secretary of Defense Donald Rumsfeld: the distinction between *known knowns*, *known unknowns*, and *unknown unknowns*. While originally coined in a military context, this framework is universally applicable to decision-making in business, investing, personal life, and any domain involving risk and complexity.

Known Knowns: What We Understand

Known knowns are the things we are aware of and understand with reasonable clarity. These are the facts, relationships, and dynamics for which we have reliable data and established models. In short, they are the parts of reality we can confidently predict and plan around.

- **Example: Physics of a pendulum.** Given the length of the string and the force applied, we can calculate its motion with high accuracy.
- **Example: Historical returns of a broad market index.** While the future is uncertain, the past average return and variance are well-documented and form a reliable baseline for probabilistic forecasting.
- **Example: Personal skills.** You know what you are capable of because you have experience, training, and track records.

Decisions in the realm of known knowns are comparatively straightforward. Because the variables are understood and the outcomes relatively predictable, we can apply deterministic planning and standard models with confidence. That said, even within known knowns, uncertainty can creep in if we overestimate our accuracy or fail to account for small perturbations.

Known Unknowns: What We Recognize but Cannot Fully Predict

Known unknowns are variables or outcomes we recognize as important but cannot measure precisely. We know they exist, but we do not know their exact values or timing. This is where probability begins to play a central role.

- **Example: Election outcomes.** Polls and trends give partial information, but no one can predict the result with certainty. Probabilistic models provide ranges of likelihoods rather than exact forecasts.
- **Example: Project completion time.** You can estimate based on past experience and known constraints, but unforeseen delays, dependencies, and inefficiencies create variability.
- **Example: Market volatility.** While historical data provides a measure of expected variance, short-term fluctuations remain unpredictable.

The key to handling known unknowns is to adopt strategies that account for variability. Scenario planning, sensitivity analysis, and stress-testing are tools that help manage these uncertainties. In practice, successful decision-makers accept that outcomes are probabilistic, preparing for multiple possibilities rather than betting everything on a single forecast.

Unknown Unknowns: The Blind Spots of Reality

Unknown unknowns are the most challenging category: risks and opportunities that we do not even know exist. These are surprises, black swans, and emergent phenomena that lie outside our current understanding. By definition, they are impossible to quantify or predict in advance.

- **Example: The 2008 financial crisis.** Few analysts foresaw the collapse of the housing market and its cascading effects. It was a systemic risk lying outside the scope of conventional models.
- **Example: Technological breakthroughs.** Innovations like the internet, smartphones, or AI have fundamentally reshaped industries in ways few could anticipate.
- **Example: Pandemics.** While scientists understand the possibility of outbreaks, the exact timing, scale, and societal impact are largely unknowable beforehand.

The best defense against unknown unknowns is not prediction, but *robustness, flexibility, and optionality.* Building systems, strategies, and habits that can absorb shocks and adapt to surprise allows you to thrive even when the unexpected occurs.

The Spectrum of Knowledge and Decision-Making

These three categories exist along a spectrum rather than as isolated buckets. Many decisions involve a mixture of all three. Consider starting a business:

- **Known knowns:** You understand your own skills, the basic economics of your product, and the market niche you aim to serve.
- **Known unknowns:** You recognize that customer adoption rates, competitive reactions, and regulatory changes are uncertain, but can estimate probabilities and plan contingencies.
- **Unknown unknowns:** You cannot anticipate disruptive technologies, sudden market crashes, or shifts in consumer behavior. These require flexible strategies and optionality.

The power of a probabilistic mindset is that it equips you to operate across this spectrum. You maximize the value of known knowns, hedge the impact of known unknowns, and build resilience against unknown unknowns. By doing so, you turn uncertainty from a source of fear into a source of opportunity.

Practical Takeaways

1. **Identify what you know.** Catalog your known knowns and use them as a foundation for action.
2. **Map your uncertainties.** Recognize known unknowns and assign probabilities or ranges where possible.
3. **Prepare for the unexpected.** Build systems, processes, and habits that are robust to unknown unknowns.
4. **Adapt your mindset.** Accept that certainty is rare; embrace flexibility, optionality, and probabilistic reasoning.
5. **Use feedback loops.** Continuously update your understanding as new information emerges, shifting items from unknown to known.

By distinguishing between what is known, what is uncertain, and what is completely beyond foresight, you gain clarity in decision-making. This framework is a cornerstone of probabilistic thinking: it teaches humility, prepares you for surprise, and provides a practical method to navigate a complex, unpredictable world.

1.3 Why Humans Resist Uncertainty

Despite the undeniable presence of uncertainty in every aspect of life, humans are wired to resist it. We crave predictability, structure, and clear outcomes even when embracing uncertainty would lead to better decisions. Understanding why we resist uncertainty is essential for cultivating a probabilistic mindset, because awareness of these tendencies allows us to counteract them deliberately.

The Psychological Comfort of Certainty

Uncertainty triggers discomfort, stress, and anxiety. Our brains are pattern-seeking machines: they crave coherence and consistency. When faced with ambiguity, we instinctively try to impose order, even when none exists. This drive has evolutionary roots:

- In early human environments, quickly recognizing patterns could mean the difference between life and death. Misjudging a predator's presence or misreading environmental signals had immediate consequences.
- Certainty reduces cognitive load. Predictable environments are easier to navigate mentally, freeing resources for other tasks.

In modern life, this instinct manifests in ways such as overconfidence in predictions, reliance on rules of thumb, and discomfort with probabilistic thinking. We prefer "I know what will happen" to "I have a range of possible outcomes with varying probabilities," even when the latter is more accurate.

Cognitive Biases That Amplify Resistance

Several well-studied cognitive biases make us particularly averse to uncertainty:

- **Overconfidence Bias:** We overestimate our knowledge and ability to predict outcomes. This leads to underestimating variability and ignoring tail risks.
- **Hindsight Bias:** After an event occurs, we perceive it as more predictable than it actually was. This reinforces the illusion that uncertainty is controllable.
- **Ambiguity Aversion:** People prefer known risks over unknown risks, even if the expected value is higher for the unknown. This can cause overly conservative decisions.
- **Illusion of Control:** We overestimate our influence over outcomes, convincing ourselves that careful planning can eliminate randomness.

These biases are not flaws they are mental shortcuts that generally help us survive and operate efficiently. The problem is that in complex, high-variance environments like markets, entrepreneurship, or long-term planning, these shortcuts often backfire.

Emotional Resistance and Fear of Loss

Uncertainty is inherently uncomfortable because it forces us to confront the possibility of loss. Prospect theory shows that humans feel the pain of loss roughly twice as strongly as the pleasure of an equivalent gain. This makes uncertainty emotionally aversive:

- Investors may avoid high-probability, high-reward opportunities because they fear short-term volatility.
- Leaders may cling to rigid plans to avoid potential criticism or perceived failure.
- Individuals may stay in jobs, relationships, or habits that are suboptimal simply because the alternative is unknown.

By recognizing this emotional wiring, we can deliberately train ourselves to tolerate ambiguity and make decisions based on probabilities rather than fear.

Cultural and Social Factors

Humans are social creatures, and societies often reinforce the desire for certainty:

- Cultural norms value predictability and penalize deviation from expectations.
- Organizations reward consistent, rule-following behavior over probabilistic experimentation.
- Social comparison encourages aligning with the majority, which reduces perceived uncertainty but may suppress better, risk-informed choices.

Understanding these pressures helps explain why even intelligent, well-educated individuals resist probabilistic thinking. The resistance is partly internal (cognitive and emotional) and partly external (cultural and social).

Overcoming the Resistance

Awareness is the first step. Probabilistic thinkers actively cultivate comfort with uncertainty by:

- **Quantifying risk:** Replacing vague fear with measurable probabilities.
- **Embracing ranges and distributions:** Accepting that multiple outcomes are possible rather than relying on a single prediction.
- **Building optionality:** Designing decisions to preserve flexibility, so that the cost of being wrong is limited.
- **Practicing exposure:** Deliberately confronting small uncertainties to build emotional resilience.
- **Using mental models:** Inversion, scenario planning, and stress testing reduce the psychological burden of unknowns.

By recognizing the cognitive, emotional, and social roots of uncertainty aversion, you can begin to rewire your thinking. Probabilistic thinking is not just a tool for making smarter decisions it is a skill that transforms your relationship with uncertainty itself, turning discomfort into clarity, hesitation into action, and fear into opportunity.

Chapter 2

Randomness vs. Risk

Imagine standing at a casino table. A roll of the dice could make you rich or leave you empty-handed. Now imagine investing in a diversified stock portfolio. Some days the market rises, other days it falls, but over time, your returns tend to follow patterns. At first glance, both scenarios seem uncertain but the nature of that uncertainty is fundamentally different.

This chapter explores the crucial distinction between *pure randomness* and *measurable risk.* Understanding this difference is central to probabilistic thinking and high-quality decision-making. Randomness is the inherent unpredictability in events with no discernible pattern, while risk is uncertainty that can be quantified, modeled, and managed.

We will also explore concepts such as variance and volatility, which describe how outcomes can fluctuate around an expected value, and the idea of viewing risk as exposure rather than as a guaranteed outcome. By the end of this chapter, you will see that while you cannot eliminate uncertainty, you can make it actionable turning probabilistic insight into strategic advantage.

2.1 Pure Randomness vs. Measurable Risk

At first glance, all uncertainty may seem the same a blur of unpredictability. But as any experienced decision-maker knows, there is a profound difference between *pure randomness* and *measurable risk.* Recognizing this distinction is essential for making high-quality decisions and avoiding the traps of overconfidence or paralysis.

Pure Randomness: Unquantifiable Uncertainty

Pure randomness refers to outcomes that are inherently unpredictable and cannot be systematically measured or modeled. These events have no discernible pattern, no historical baseline, and no reliable probability distribution that you can trust. They are, by definition, unknowable before they occur.

- **Example: Lottery numbers.** Each draw is independent, with equal probability for all numbers. No amount of observation or analysis can increase your odds beyond the baseline.
- **Example: Natural disasters in unpredictable locations.** While scientists can estimate probabilities in broad terms, the exact timing and impact of events like earthquakes or tornadoes remain largely random.
- **Example: Short-term market noise.** Individual stock price movements over minutes or hours often reflect random fluctuations in sentiment, news, or liquidity, making precise prediction impossible.

Pure randomness is difficult to manage directly. The best strategies involve diversification, hedging, and designing systems that are resilient to the unknown, rather than trying to predict or control the outcome.

Measurable Risk: Uncertainty You Can Quantify

Measurable risk, in contrast, refers to uncertainty that can be estimated, modeled, and managed using data, probabilities, and historical patterns. While the outcome is not guaranteed, the likelihood of various outcomes can be assessed, allowing for informed decision-making.

- **Example: Insurance policies.** Insurers use historical data to calculate the probability of events like car accidents or fire damage, allowing them to price coverage appropriately.
- **Example: Investment portfolios.** By analyzing historical returns, correlations, and volatility, investors can estimate expected outcomes and balance risk versus reward.
- **Example: Project planning.** Techniques like Monte Carlo simulations allow managers to assess the likelihood of meeting deadlines, accounting for variable dependencies and potential delays.

Measurable risk allows for active management. Decision-makers can hedge against downside, allocate resources strategically, and make probabilistic bets with known expected value. Unlike pure randomness, measurable risk is actionable it can be mitigated, optimized, or exploited.

The Crucial Distinction

The distinction between pure randomness and measurable risk is subtle but profound:

- **Predictability:** Measurable risk exists within known probability distributions; pure randomness defies prediction.
- **Actionability:** Measurable risk can be managed through hedging, diversification, and strategic positioning; pure randomness cannot be controlled, only absorbed.
- **Decision-making:** Probabilistic thinking applies most effectively to measurable risk. Treating pure randomness as if it were predictable is a common source of errors and overconfidence.

Practical Implications for Decision-Makers

Understanding this distinction transforms how you approach decisions in every domain:

- **Investing:** Focus on systems with measurable risk rather than trying to predict pure randomness in the short term. Accept that daily price movements are largely noise.
- **Entrepreneurship:** Evaluate business decisions probabilistically identify risks that can be quantified and managed while acknowledging areas of true uncertainty.
- **Life Planning:** Recognize which uncertainties can be modeled (career growth probabilities, education returns) versus those that cannot (random accidents, sudden societal shifts) and design flexibility into your plans.

In essence, pure randomness is the uncontrollable backdrop of life a force to respect and absorb while measurable risk is the realm where skill, strategy, and probabilistic thinking create advantage. Distinguishing between the two allows you to act decisively, allocate resources wisely, and convert uncertainty into opportunity rather than fear.

2.2 Variance and Volatility

Once we distinguish between pure randomness and measurable risk, the next step is to understand how outcomes can fluctuate around an expected result. Two of the most important concepts in this regard are *variance* and *volatility*. Both describe the degree of uncertainty in outcomes, but they serve slightly different purposes in decision-making and risk management.

Variance: Quantifying the Spread of Outcomes

Variance is a statistical measure that captures how much a set of possible outcomes deviates from the expected value. In simpler terms, it tells us how widely results can scatter around the average. A high variance indicates that outcomes are spread out and unpredictable, while a low variance suggests consistency and predictability.

- **Example: Investment returns.** Consider two stocks with an expected annual return of 8%. Stock A fluctuates between 7% and 9%, while Stock B swings between -10% and 26%. Both have the same expected return, but Stock B has much higher variance, meaning it is far less predictable in the short term.

- **Example: Project completion times.** A task expected to take 30 days could be completed in 29–31 days (low variance) or 20–50 days (high variance). High variance introduces uncertainty that must be accounted for in planning.

Variance is a fundamental building block for probabilistic thinking. It quantifies uncertainty in numerical terms, allowing decision-makers to compare options not just by their expected outcome, but by how reliable or volatile those outcomes are.

Volatility: Dynamic Fluctuations Over Time

Volatility is a concept closely related to variance but often applied in time-series contexts, such as financial markets or operational processes. While variance measures the overall dispersion of outcomes, volatility focuses on the magnitude and frequency of fluctuations over a specific period.

- **Example: Stock market.** A stock with daily price swings of $\pm 0.5\%$ is less volatile than one that moves $\pm 5\%$ daily, even if their long-term expected returns are the same. High volatility implies that short-term outcomes can deviate significantly from the average.

- **Example: Business revenue.** A company experiencing quarterly revenue swings due to seasonality or demand shocks exhibits high volatility, which may affect cash flow planning and risk exposure.

Volatility is particularly important because it impacts psychological and practical aspects of decision-making. Humans are sensitive to swings, and high volatility can trigger stress, poor judgment, or overreaction. Probabilistic thinking helps us distinguish between normal fluctuations and true systemic risk.

Why Variance and Volatility Matter

Understanding variance and volatility is essential for navigating risk intelligently:

- **Decision-making under uncertainty:** Options with the same expected value can have vastly different risk profiles. By analyzing variance, you can choose paths aligned with your risk tolerance and strategic objectives.
- **Portfolio construction:** Investors use variance and volatility to diversify and balance portfolios, minimizing the chance of extreme negative outcomes while capturing upside potential.
- **Stress-testing and scenario planning:** Knowing the potential range of outcomes allows individuals and organizations to prepare contingency plans and buffers for extreme events.
- **Cognitive resilience:** Awareness of natural variability helps prevent overreaction to short-term fluctuations, improving long-term decision quality.

Variance, Volatility, and Probabilistic Thinking

In probabilistic terms, variance and volatility are measures of uncertainty that allow us to quantify and compare different outcomes. They transform abstract uncertainty into actionable insight:

- High variance or volatility signals that outcomes are widely spread, requiring hedges, optionality, or risk mitigation.
- Low variance or volatility indicates more predictable outcomes, suitable for strategies that rely on steady progress or accumulation.
- By combining expected value with variance or volatility, we gain a richer understanding of the *risk-reward profile* of any decision.

Ultimately, variance and volatility are not obstacles to decision-making; they are tools for smarter navigation. Recognizing how outcomes can fluctuate and preparing accordingly allows you to act decisively, manage exposure, and exploit opportunities, even in the presence of uncertainty. These concepts bridge the gap between theory and practical action, forming a core part of the probabilistic mindset.

2.3 Risk as Exposure, Not Outcome

A common mistake in thinking about risk is to equate it with negative outcomes. Many people define risk as "the chance something bad will happen" and treat it as a binary event: either you succeed or you fail. In reality, risk is not the outcome itself it is the *exposure* to uncertain events. This distinction is crucial for developing a probabilistic mindset and making smarter decisions.

Understanding Risk as Exposure

Risk measures your potential for loss or gain in the presence of uncertainty. It is fundamentally about the range of possible outcomes you might experience and the degree to which you are vulnerable or positioned to benefit. By focusing on exposure rather than actual outcomes, you shift from reactive thinking to proactive management.

- **Example: Investment portfolios.** Owning stocks exposes you to the risk of price fluctuations. If the market declines, you may lose money; if it rises, you may gain. The risk lies in your exposure, not the fact that the market moves.
- **Example: Entrepreneurship.** Starting a business exposes you to revenue volatility, operational challenges, and competitive pressures. Risk is present from the outset, regardless of whether you ultimately succeed or fail.
- **Example: Health decisions.** Choosing to exercise or adopt a new diet exposes you to certain risks (injury, overtraining) but also potential gains (fitness, longevity). The risk is in the exposure, not the eventual outcome.

By viewing risk as exposure, you can separate *process* from *results*. Good probabilistic decision-making focuses on optimizing exposure to favorable outcomes while limiting vulnerability to catastrophic losses.

The Fallacy of Outcome-Based Thinking

Focusing solely on outcomes leads to two common errors:

1. **Outcome bias:** Judging a decision as good or bad based on its result rather than the quality of the decision-making process. A risky investment that pays off might seem wise, even if the underlying probability was low. Conversely, a well-structured decision could fail due to random events, even though it was strategically sound.

2. **Short-term myopia:** Reacting to immediate results without considering exposure over time. Frequent small losses or gains may mask the underlying risk profile, leading to overconfidence or panic.

Outcome-based thinking can make people overly cautious or dangerously reckless, because it confuses luck with skill and fails to account for the probabilistic nature of the world.

Measuring and Managing Exposure

When risk is understood as exposure, it becomes actionable. Decision-makers can quantify, limit, and optimize risk through several methods:

- **Diversification:** Spreading exposure across multiple independent opportunities reduces the impact of any single negative event.
- **Position sizing:** Allocating resources proportional to the expected risk ensures that a single adverse outcome does not threaten the entire system.
- **Hedging:** Using derivatives, insurance, or contingency plans to mitigate exposure to high-impact events.
- **Optionality:** Maintaining flexibility to adapt to new information or unforeseen events reduces net exposure while preserving upside potential.

Each of these strategies focuses on controlling exposure rather than trying to predict or avoid every negative outcome a core principle of probabilistic thinking.

Practical Insights

Understanding risk as exposure offers several critical advantages:

- **Process over luck:** You can evaluate decisions based on whether they appropriately manage exposure, independent of short-term outcomes.
- **Long-term consistency:** By optimizing exposure, you increase the probability of favorable results over time, even in highly uncertain environments.
- **Resilience:** Systems designed around exposure can absorb shocks and rare events without catastrophic failure, embodying the principle of anti-fragility.

- **Opportunity recognition:** Seeing risk as exposure allows you to identify asymmetric bets situations where the upside greatly outweighs the downside a hallmark of high-probability, high-value decision-making.

In probabilistic thinking, risk is not an enemy to be feared, nor an outcome to be avoided. It is a signal: a measure of how exposed you are to the unpredictable forces of reality. By managing exposure intelligently, you can transform uncertainty from a source of anxiety into a lever for advantage. This perspective shifts the focus from luck or fate to deliberate, disciplined action, which is the essence of mastery in a probabilistic world.

Chapter 3

Systems, Complexity Variance

Imagine a forest ecosystem: trees grow, animals hunt, rivers flow, and seasons change. Every element interacts with others in ways that are sometimes predictable, often surprising. A small change a new species, a drought, or a storm can ripple across the system in unexpected ways.

This chapter explores the intricate dynamics of complex systems, where outcomes are rarely proportional to inputs and small events can trigger massive consequences. In such systems, variance is not just a statistical measure; it is a reflection of the hidden interconnections, feedback loops, and potential for extreme events.

We will examine *complex adaptive systems*, where agents interact and adapt in unpredictable ways; *non-linear effects and feedback loops*, which can amplify or dampen outcomes; and the concept of *tail risks and black swans*, which represent rare but catastrophic events that conventional models often fail to anticipate.

Understanding these principles is essential for probabilistic thinking, because it allows you to navigate environments where simple cause-and-effect reasoning fails, and where resilience, optionality, and strategic flexibility become the keys to survival and advantage.

3.1 Complex Adaptive Systems

The world is not composed of isolated events; it is a web of interconnected agents, each influencing and responding to one another. These webs whether ecosystems, economies, or organizations are what we call *complex adaptive systems* (CAS). Understanding CAS is crucial for anyone seeking to make decisions in an uncertain, high-variance environment.

Defining Complex Adaptive Systems

A complex adaptive system is a collection of interacting agents, each of which follows simple rules, adapts based on experience, and responds to changes in the environment. Unlike linear systems, where inputs produce predictable outputs, CAS exhibit emergent behavior: the whole is greater than the sum of its parts.

- **Ecosystems:** Plants, animals, microorganisms, and the environment interact in ways that maintain balance but can shift dramatically due to small perturbations.
- **Economies:** Consumers, businesses, regulators, and markets co-evolve. A minor policy change or innovation can cascade through the system with far-reaching effects.
- **Organizations:** Employees, teams, and leaders interact dynamically. Informal networks, feedback, and adaptive behavior often determine success more than formal structures.

These systems are characterized by adaptation, interdependence, and non-linearity. Small actions can produce disproportionately large outcomes, and outcomes often cannot be traced to a single cause.

Key Properties of Complex Adaptive Systems

Understanding the behavior of CAS requires recognizing several key properties:

1. **Emergence:** Patterns and behaviors emerge from local interactions, rather than being imposed from above. For example, traffic jams form spontaneously from individual driving behaviors, without centralized coordination.
2. **Adaptation:** Agents learn and adjust based on experience. In financial markets, traders respond to price signals, which in turn influence the market itself.
3. **Non-linearity:** Small changes can have outsized effects, and large interventions can have minimal impact, making prediction extremely difficult.
4. **Interconnectedness:** Elements of the system are interdependent. A disruption in one area can cascade across the system in unexpected ways.
5. **Feedback Loops:** Positive and negative feedback amplifies or dampens behaviors. A viral social media post is a clear example of positive feedback, while regulatory mechanisms often act as negative feedback to restore balance.

Why CAS Matters in Decision-Making

Traditional linear thinking assumes that cause and effect are proportional and predictable. In complex adaptive systems, this assumption fails. Probabilistic thinking is essential because it allows decision-makers to account for variability, interconnectedness, and emergent behavior.

- **Risk is systemic, not isolated:** A single failure can ripple throughout the system, creating unexpected consequences.
- **Small interventions can have large impacts:** Strategic positioning and leverage often outperform brute-force approaches.
- **Predictive models have limits:** While forecasting is possible in narrow, stable domains, CAS require flexibility, optionality, and adaptive strategies.

Examples of Complex Adaptive Systems in Action

- **Financial Markets:** Traders, institutions, and regulators continuously interact, producing emergent market behaviors. Flash crashes, bubbles, and systemic crises are products of these interactions.
- **Urban Systems:** Cities evolve as residents, businesses, transportation, and infrastructure interact. Small policy changes or innovations can dramatically reshape traffic flow, housing markets, or social dynamics.
- **Biological Systems:** The human immune system adapts to pathogens dynamically. Vaccination, environmental changes, and microbial evolution interact in complex ways that are not entirely predictable.

Practical Lessons for Navigating CAS

Understanding CAS changes how we approach uncertainty and risk:

- Focus on **adaptive strategies** rather than fixed plans. Systems evolve; your decisions must evolve with them.
- Build **redundancy and optionality** to absorb shocks. Multiple pathways to success increase resilience.
- Monitor **feedback loops** and early warning signals. Small changes in key nodes can indicate larger systemic shifts.

- Embrace **emergent patterns** rather than attempting to control every variable. Predicting exact outcomes is often futile; understanding dynamics is key.

Complex adaptive systems remind us that the world is interconnected, dynamic, and often unpredictable. By recognizing the emergent, adaptive, and non-linear nature of these systems, we can move from reactive, deterministic thinking to a probabilistic, strategic mindset one that leverages complexity rather than being trapped by it.

3.2 Non-Linear Effects and Feedback Loops

In complex systems, cause and effect are rarely proportional. Small actions can produce disproportionately large outcomes, while seemingly massive interventions may barely move the needle. This phenomenon is called *non-linearity*, and it is often intertwined with *feedback loops*, which amplify or dampen changes within a system. Understanding these dynamics is essential for navigating uncertainty and making decisions that account for systemic behavior.

Non-Linear Effects: When Small Causes Trigger Big Consequences

Non-linearity occurs when the relationship between inputs and outputs is not a straight line. In other words, doubling the effort does not necessarily double the result. Instead, small perturbations can cascade into massive effects, or large interventions may have minimal impact.

- **Example: Social networks.** A single tweet by an influential figure can go viral and influence millions, while thousands of ordinary posts may go unnoticed.
- **Example: Markets.** A minor policy change or unexpected news item can trigger widespread market fluctuations far beyond the initial event.
- **Example: Ecosystems.** Introducing a small new species to an environment can dramatically alter predator-prey dynamics, resulting in unforeseen population shifts.

Non-linearity teaches us that not all actions are created equal. Strategic leverage targeting key nodes or critical points can produce outsized results. Conversely, ignoring the non-linear nature of a system can lead to underestimating risks or overestimating control.

Feedback Loops: Amplifying and Damping Forces

Feedback loops describe situations where outputs of a system feed back into its inputs, influencing future behavior. There are two primary types:

1. **Positive Feedback Loops:** These amplify change and can lead to exponential growth or collapse.
    - Example: Viral marketing. As more people share a product, its visibility increases, attracting even more shares.
    - Example: Financial bubbles. Rising prices attract more buyers, which drives prices even higher until the bubble bursts.
2. **Negative Feedback Loops:** These stabilize systems by counteracting change.
    - Example: Thermostat regulation. A room that gets too hot triggers cooling, bringing temperature back to equilibrium.
    - Example: Population dynamics. When a prey population increases, predators have more food, which eventually reduces the prey population, maintaining balance.

Feedback loops are critical to understanding system behavior because they determine whether changes are amplified, dampened, or oscillate unpredictably.

Non-Linearity and Feedback Loops in Decision-Making

Recognizing non-linear effects and feedback loops allows probabilistic thinkers to:

- Identify points of leverage where small, informed actions can have outsized impact.
- Avoid underestimating risks that may be amplified through positive feedback loops.
- Design systems and strategies that exploit beneficial loops while dampening harmful ones.
- Appreciate that outcomes are rarely proportional to inputs, making flexible, adaptive strategies more effective than rigid plans.

Examples in Practice

- **Economics:** Interest rate changes can trigger non-linear reactions in credit markets, amplified through feedback loops in investor behavior.

- **Technology adoption:** Early adopters influence mainstream adoption, creating exponential growth curves.
- **Health systems:** Small improvements in hygiene or vaccination can dramatically reduce disease spread due to feedback in infection rates.

In essence, non-linear effects and feedback loops are the invisible forces that determine whether systems spiral out of control, stabilize, or grow exponentially. By understanding and anticipating these forces, you can design decisions and strategies that harness systemic dynamics, rather than being blindsided by them a core principle of probabilistic thinking in complex environments.

3.3 Tail Risks and Black Swans

In most systems, whether financial markets, ecosystems, or social networks, the majority of events cluster around expected outcomes. We often assume that extremes are rare and manageable, but history and complex system behavior tell a different story. Occasionally, highly improbable events occur events so rare and impactful that they can reshape entire industries, societies, or ecosystems. These are what we call *tail risks*, and when they are surprising, difficult to predict, and retrospectively rationalized, they are known as *Black Swan events*, a term popularized by Nassim Nicholas Taleb.

Tail Risks: Low Probability, High Impact

Tail risks occupy the extreme ends of probability distributions. While they occur infrequently, their consequences can be catastrophic or transformational. Unlike ordinary fluctuations, tail risks dominate the overall risk profile of complex systems. Understanding and preparing for them is a hallmark of probabilistic thinking.

- **Financial markets:** The 2008 global financial crisis, triggered by the collapse of the subprime mortgage market, was a tail event that few models predicted. Its ripple effects impacted banks, governments, and economies worldwide.
- **Natural disasters:** Major earthquakes, hurricanes, or tsunamis happen rarely, but when they do, the damage to life, infrastructure, and economies is immense.
- **Technological shocks:** A sudden cyberattack on critical infrastructure or the failure of a widely-used technology platform can produce outsized consequences far beyond ordinary expectations.

Tail risks illustrate that extreme outcomes, though improbable, often contribute more to long-term variability than the "normal" events we typically focus on.

The Black Swan Phenomenon

Black Swan events are a special subset of tail risks, defined by three essential characteristics:

1. **Rarity:** They lie outside the realm of regular expectations and are usually considered nearly impossible before they occur.
2. **Extreme impact:** Their consequences can be transformative, leading to systemic failures, paradigm shifts, or massive opportunities.
3. **Retrospective predictability:** After the event occurs, people often rationalize it as if it could have been anticipated, ignoring the inherent unpredictability that existed beforehand.

The Black Swan concept challenges deterministic thinking and conventional risk models, reminding us that uncertainty is often underappreciated and mismeasured.

Managing Tail Risks

While the precise timing and nature of tail events cannot be predicted, exposure to them can be managed through careful planning and strategic design:

- **Diversification:** Spread exposure across uncorrelated assets, systems, or opportunities to reduce the impact of any single catastrophic event.
- **Optionality:** Maintain multiple pathways and choices that allow you to benefit from positive tail events while limiting downside.
- **Hedging:** Use insurance, derivatives, or contingency reserves to protect against extreme negative outcomes.
- **Stress-testing:** Scenario analysis under extreme conditions helps identify vulnerabilities and prepare mitigation strategies before disasters strike.

Managing tail risk is less about predicting the unpredictable and more about designing systems and decisions that are robust, resilient, and adaptive to extremes.

Probabilistic Thinking and Tail Events

Tail risks and Black Swan events are a powerful reminder of why a probabilistic mindset is essential:

- Focus on **resilience and adaptive strategies**, rather than relying on precise forecasts.
- Seek **asymmetric opportunities**, where the potential upside greatly outweighs downside exposure.
- Maintain **awareness of systemic interconnections**, understanding how extreme events propagate through complex adaptive systems.
- Accept that **uncertainty is inherent**, and designing for variability is a more reliable path than trying to eliminate risk.

In complex systems, the rare events often matter more than the common ones. Tail risks dominate long-term outcomes, and Black Swan events challenge our assumptions about predictability. By acknowledging these realities and building strategies around exposure, optionality, and resilience, you transform uncertainty from a source of fear into a lever for strategic advantage. This perspective is not merely defensive it is a core principle of probabilistic thinking that allows you to thrive in a world defined by unpredictability.

Chapter 4

Base Rates Expected Value

Imagine you are considering an investment opportunity recommended by a charismatic entrepreneur. They tell you that similar ventures have yielded enormous returns, and their pitch is compelling. But before committing your capital, a crucial question arises: how often do such ventures actually succeed? How much of the story is luck, hype, or selective reporting?

This chapter explores two fundamental tools that help navigate uncertainty: *base rates* and *expected value*. Base rates provide the statistical backdrop against which individual claims should be assessed, reminding us that anecdotes and personal stories are often misleading. Expected value translates probabilities into actionable guidance, allowing us to make decisions that maximize long-term outcomes rather than being swayed by immediate appearances.

We will examine why ignoring base rates leads to common errors, how expected value functions as a decision compass, and the difference between positive and negative expectancy decisions. Together, these concepts form a critical foundation for probabilistic thinking and high-quality decision-making.

4.1 Why Base Rates Matter More Than Anecdotes

Human beings are natural storytellers. We are wired to notice individual cases, compelling narratives, and vivid examples. A friend's spectacular investment win, a viral success story, or a striking personal experience often captures our attention far more than abstract statistics. Yet this cognitive bias can lead to serious errors in judgment. In probabilistic thinking, one of the most essential tools to counteract these biases is the *base rate*.

What is a Base Rate?

A base rate is the underlying probability of an event occurring within a relevant population, independent of specific anecdotal information. It represents the historical or statistical norm the "background frequency" of outcomes that provides context for decision-making.

For example:

- In venture capital, the base rate of startup failure is around 90%. Even if one entrepreneur presents a compelling pitch and cites other successful startups, the base rate reminds us that failure is far more common than success.
- In medical diagnostics, if a disease affects 1 in 1,000 people, a positive test result must be interpreted against this base rate. Ignoring it can lead to false alarms or unnecessary interventions.

Base rates anchor our expectations in reality, preventing us from being swayed by outliers or emotionally charged anecdotes.

The Danger of Anecdotal Thinking

Anecdotes are vivid, memorable, and persuasive. They often suggest patterns that do not exist or exaggerate the probability of rare events. Humans are particularly susceptible to:

- **Availability bias:** We judge events as more likely if they are easy to recall or emotionally striking. A single high-profile success story can make similar ventures appear more probable than they really are.
- **Representativeness heuristic:** We assume that specific cases reflect the general population, ignoring statistical realities. A charismatic founder may seem representative of successful entrepreneurs, even if most founders fail.
- **Confirmation bias:** We selectively notice anecdotes that support our desired outcome while dismissing contradictory evidence.

Relying solely on anecdotes is a form of probabilistic myopia: it ignores the statistical backdrop that governs reality and increases the likelihood of costly mistakes.

Base Rates as Probabilistic Anchors

In probabilistic decision-making, base rates serve as anchors that keep assessments grounded. They are particularly important when evaluating rare events, high-variance outcomes, or situations with incomplete information.

- **Example: Startup investing.** Knowing that only 10% of startups succeed helps investors calibrate expectations, structure portfolios, and avoid overconcentration in high-risk ventures.
- **Example: Hiring decisions.** Historical performance data of candidates from a particular school, industry, or background provides a base rate that helps distinguish signal from anecdotal noise.
- **Example: Personal decisions.** When considering lifestyle choices, such as adopting a new diet or training program, base rates derived from broad populations help separate genuine patterns from individual stories.

By comparing individual cases to base rates, we can evaluate whether a specific claim is unusually likely or merely conforms to statistical norms.

Integrating Base Rates with Specific Information

Base rates are not meant to replace context or specific information; rather, they must be integrated with it using probabilistic reasoning. Bayesian thinking formalizes this process: starting with the base rate (prior probability), we update it as we receive new evidence, balancing anecdotal signals against statistical reality.

- **Example: Medical diagnosis.** A rare disease has a base rate of 1 in 1,000. A positive test result increases the probability of the disease, but the base rate ensures that the likelihood remains low unless corroborated by additional evidence.
- **Example: Investing.** A startup founder may cite early traction or market trends, but the base rate of success for similar ventures informs whether this traction truly increases the odds of success.

The combination of base rates and specific evidence allows for rational, probabilistic decision-making that avoids the pitfalls of anecdotal overconfidence.

Practical Lessons

- Always start with the base rate before evaluating specific claims or anecdotes.
- Use anecdotes as additional information, not as the sole basis for decisions.
- Be aware of cognitive biases that amplify the influence of vivid stories over statistical reality.

- Apply Bayesian updating: adjust base rates in light of new, credible evidence, but never ignore the underlying probabilities.

In short, base rates are the probabilistic compass that keeps decision-making grounded in reality. Anecdotes are compelling, but without reference to statistical norms, they can mislead, distort judgment, and increase exposure to unnecessary risk. Mastering the ability to balance base rates with specific evidence is a cornerstone of probabilistic thinking, providing clarity amid uncertainty and guiding decisions toward long-term, high-expectancy outcomes.

4.2 Expected Value as a Decision Compass

Every decision we make involves trade-offs, even if we are not consciously aware of them. Will you invest in a startup, change careers, or try a new strategy in the stock market? Each choice carries potential outcomes with varying probabilities and magnitudes of gain or loss. Expected value (EV) provides a mathematical framework for navigating these choices a probabilistic compass that helps guide decisions toward long-term advantage.

What is Expected Value?

Expected value is the weighted average of all possible outcomes of a decision, where each outcome is multiplied by its probability. In essence, it tells us what we can "expect" to gain or lose on average if we repeat the decision many times.

Mathematically:

$$EV = \sum_i P_i \times V_i$$

where P_i is the probability of outcome i and V_i is the value (gain or loss) associated with that outcome.

- **Positive EV:** On average, the decision will yield a net gain over repeated trials.
- **Negative EV:** On average, the decision will yield a net loss over repeated trials.

EV is not about predicting what will happen in a single instance; it is about aligning your decisions with long-term probabilistic advantage.

Expected Value in Everyday Decisions

Expected value applies far beyond formal finance or gambling scenarios. Consider these examples:

- **Startup investing:** Suppose a venture has a 10% chance of generating \$1,000,000 and a 90% chance of losing \$100,000. The expected value is:

  $$EV = 0.1 \times 1,000,000 + 0.9 \times (-100,000) = 100,000 - 90,000 = 10,000$$

  Despite a high probability of loss, the positive EV indicates a favorable bet from a probabilistic perspective.

- **Insurance:** Paying a small premium to protect against a catastrophic event has negative EV from a purely monetary perspective but positive EV in terms of risk-adjusted utility. Probabilistic thinking incorporates both financial and subjective value.

- **Personal choices:** Choosing to invest time in learning a skill may have a low immediate payoff but high probability of compounding benefits in the long term a positive EV decision in career or personal growth.

EV vs. Anecdotal Success

A common trap is evaluating a decision by its most visible outcome rather than its expected value. Just because a friend made a fortune investing in a risky stock does not mean the bet had positive EV. Probabilistic thinking separates short-term luck from decisions that are advantageous on average over many trials.

- Focus on the **average outcome over time**, not a single anecdotal result.
- Understand that high variance may obscure expected value in the short term. A positive EV decision can fail multiple times before yielding a win.
- Use expected value to prioritize decisions that are **systematically profitable**, rather than emotionally appealing.

Expected Value and Decision Strategy

EV is most powerful when combined with other probabilistic tools:

- **Base rates:** Accurately estimating probabilities requires knowledge of historical norms and statistical frequencies.
- **Variance and risk assessment:** High EV does not guarantee safety; understanding potential downsides allows for better risk management.

- **Optionality:** Decisions with small downside and large upside create asymmetry, maximizing expected value with limited risk.

In strategic decision-making, EV transforms abstract probabilities into actionable guidance. It encourages a disciplined approach: place bets with positive expected value, avoid repeated negative EV actions, and focus on outcomes that compound advantage over time.

Practical Takeaways

- Evaluate all potential outcomes and their probabilities before making a decision.
- Translate subjective or anecdotal judgments into probabilistic estimates wherever possible.
- Focus on long-term expected value rather than immediate results.
- Combine EV with optionality and base rates to maximize advantage in uncertain environments.

Expected value is the compass that keeps probabilistic decision-making on course. By quantifying the potential payoff and risk of every action, it allows you to navigate uncertainty strategically. Over time, consistently favoring positive EV decisions compounds into significant advantage, turning probabilistic thinking from an abstract concept into a practical tool for success in life, business, and investment.

4.3 Positive vs. Negative Expectancy Decisions

In probabilistic thinking, not all decisions are created equal. Some choices, even if they occasionally fail, increase long-term advantage, while others, despite occasional wins, systematically erode it. Understanding the distinction between *positive* and *negative expectancy* decisions is critical for navigating uncertainty and building consistent success over time.

Defining Expectancy

Expectancy measures the average outcome of a decision when repeated over many trials. It incorporates both the probability of success and the magnitude of gain or loss. Formally:

$$\text{Expectancy} = \sum_i P_i \times V_i$$

where P_i is the probability of outcome i and V_i is its associated value. A positive expectancy means that, on average, the decision adds value over repeated execution. A negative expectancy indicates the opposite: repeated choices erode resources or advantage over time.

Positive Expectancy Decisions

Positive expectancy decisions are those in which the potential benefits, weighted by their probabilities, outweigh the potential losses. Even if such a decision occasionally results in a setback, it is advantageous over the long term.

- **Example: Investing with asymmetric risk-reward.** A startup investment with a 10% chance of generating $1,000,000 and a 90% chance of losing $50,000 has positive expectancy. Repeated similar bets yield net gains over time, despite many individual failures.
- **Example: Learning and skill-building.** Investing time in acquiring a high-value skill may have uncertain immediate results, but the long-term payoff consistently outweighs the short-term cost.
- **Example: Probabilistic trading strategies.** A strategy with a slight edge and disciplined risk management may win only 60% of trades but yield overall positive expectancy due to the size of the wins relative to losses.

Positive expectancy decisions are the backbone of probabilistic thinking. They are not guarantees of immediate success, but they maximize cumulative advantage over time.

Negative Expectancy Decisions

Negative expectancy decisions, in contrast, are those in which expected losses outweigh potential gains. Even occasional wins cannot compensate for the systematic erosion of advantage these decisions produce.

- **Example: Over-leveraged speculation.** Risking large sums on highly volatile assets without a favorable probability structure may occasionally pay off but is expected to lose money over time.
- **Example: Emotional decision-making.** Making career or investment choices based on fear, greed, or social pressure often results in repeated negative expectancy outcomes.
- **Example: Ignoring base rates.** Betting on rare "success stories" without accounting for historical probabilities typically leads to losses over repeated trials.

Recognizing negative expectancy decisions is vital because they silently destroy long-term compounding advantage. Avoiding them is as important as actively seeking positive expectancy opportunities.

The Role of Risk, Variance, and Optionality

Positive and negative expectancy decisions are intimately tied to risk, variance, and optionality:

- **Risk management:** Even a positive expectancy decision can fail if risk is poorly controlled. Limiting downside preserves the long-term edge.
- **Variance:** High-variance decisions may obscure expectancy in the short term. Patience and repetition reveal true expected outcomes.
- **Optionality:** Decisions with flexible paths and asymmetric payoffs increase positive expectancy by allowing upside to compound while limiting downside exposure.

Understanding these elements enables smarter decision-making under uncertainty, ensuring that your actions consistently work in your favor over time.

Practical Lessons

- Prioritize positive expectancy decisions and avoid negative expectancy traps.
- Focus on long-term cumulative advantage, not short-term results.
- Combine base rates, expected value, and risk management to identify decisions with the highest positive expectancy.
- Use probabilistic thinking to recognize patterns where consistent small advantages compound into significant long-term gains.

In essence, the distinction between positive and negative expectancy decisions is a core principle of probabilistic thinking. By identifying and consistently executing high-expectancy actions while avoiding negative ones, you build a decision-making framework that thrives under uncertainty, maximizes long-term gains, and turns probabilistic insight into tangible advantage.

Chapter 5

Cognitive Biases Against Probability

Even when we understand probabilities and base rates, our brains often betray us. Human cognition evolved to prioritize speed, pattern recognition, and emotional responses over statistical accuracy. This is why people repeatedly fall prey to predictable errors when judging risk, uncertainty, and likelihood.

This chapter explores the most common cognitive biases that sabotage probabilistic thinking. Overconfidence can make us underestimate risk, while hindsight bias convinces us that outcomes were predictable all along. The gambler's fallacy and clustering illusion trick us into seeing patterns where none exist. Loss aversion and probability neglect distort our perception of gains and risks, causing us to make decisions that are systematically suboptimal.

By understanding these biases, you can recognize when your intuition is misleading you, and apply strategies to mitigate their influence. Mastery over these mental pitfalls is essential for cultivating a truly probabilistic mindset.

5.1 Overconfidence & Hindsight Bias

One of the most persistent obstacles to probabilistic thinking is the human tendency to overestimate our knowledge, abilities, and predictive powers. This bias manifests in two interrelated ways: *overconfidence* and *hindsight bias.* Both distort our understanding of risk, probability, and uncertainty, often leading to costly errors.

Overconfidence

Overconfidence is the systematic overestimation of one's knowledge, skill, or control over outcomes. It is one of the most studied and robust cognitive biases in psychology, finance, and decision science. People who are overconfident tend to:

- Believe their predictions are more accurate than they actually are.
- Underestimate the probability of negative outcomes.
- Overcommit to high-risk decisions based on flawed confidence rather than evidence.

Examples of Overconfidence:

- **Investing:** Traders may believe they can consistently beat the market, ignoring historical evidence that even professional investors struggle to outperform benchmarks over time.
- **Entrepreneurship:** Founders often overestimate market demand, resource availability, or their team's capabilities, leading to high failure rates.
- **Forecasting:** Experts across fields from economics to politics routinely express greater certainty than warranted by data, producing forecasts that frequently miss the mark.

Overconfidence is dangerous because it amplifies exposure to risk. When we believe we are "sure," we may ignore base rates, undervalue probabilistic outcomes, and make decisions that have negative expectancy over time.

Hindsight Bias

Hindsight bias, sometimes called the "I-knew-it-all-along" effect, is our tendency to see events as more predictable after they have occurred. This bias interacts with overconfidence, reinforcing false beliefs about our ability to forecast the future.

Key characteristics of hindsight bias:

- **Retrospective predictability:** Once an outcome is known, we overestimate how predictable it was beforehand.
- **Illusion of inevitability:** Past events appear as if they had to happen, even if they were highly uncertain.
- **Misattribution of skill:** Successes are often credited to foresight rather than luck, while failures are blamed on unforeseen circumstances.

Examples of Hindsight Bias:

- **Financial markets:** After a stock market crash, analysts and commentators often claim the signals were obvious, ignoring the inherent uncertainty that existed beforehand.
- **Historical events:** Wars, political upheavals, and technological breakthroughs are frequently portrayed as "predictable," even though they were uncertain in real time.
- **Personal decisions:** Individuals often overestimate how well they could have anticipated the outcome of past choices, leading to overconfidence in future decisions.

Hindsight bias is particularly insidious because it retroactively validates overconfidence. When we perceive past outcomes as predictable, we reinforce the illusion that we can predict future events with similar accuracy.

Implications for Probabilistic Thinking

Overconfidence and hindsight bias both undermine rational probabilistic reasoning:

- They lead us to **underestimate uncertainty** and overweight our perceived predictive ability.
- They encourage **overcommitment to high-risk actions** without properly accounting for probability distributions or base rates.
- They distort learning, because successes appear inevitable and failures appear anomalous, preventing accurate calibration of future expectations.

Strategies to Mitigate These Biases

- **Use probabilistic frameworks:** Express beliefs in terms of probabilities rather than certainties.
- **Track predictions:** Keep a record of forecasts and outcomes to objectively assess accuracy over time.
- **Incorporate base rates:** Always compare specific predictions against historical frequencies to ground expectations in reality.
- **Seek disconfirming evidence:** Challenge assumptions and actively look for reasons your predictions might be wrong.

- **Apply pre-mortems:** Imagine potential failure scenarios before making decisions to counteract overconfidence and reduce hindsight illusions.

In summary, overconfidence and hindsight bias are powerful cognitive traps that distort probability perception and decision-making. Awareness and active mitigation are essential for cultivating a probabilistic mindset. By acknowledging our limitations, grounding expectations in data, and regularly updating beliefs, we can make smarter decisions under uncertainty and reduce costly mistakes that arise from the illusion of certainty.

5.2 Gambler's Fallacy & Clustering Illusion

Our brains are hardwired to detect patterns, even in randomness. While pattern recognition is crucial for learning and survival, it often misleads us when applied to probabilistic events. Two closely related biases the *gambler's fallacy* and the *clustering illusion* illustrate how humans misinterpret randomness, leading to poor decisions and exaggerated perceptions of control.

The Gambler's Fallacy

The gambler's fallacy occurs when people believe that past random events influence future ones in independent trials. This leads to the mistaken assumption that a sequence of outcomes "balances out" over short periods.

Examples:

- **Casino games:** If a roulette wheel lands on red five times in a row, a gambler might believe that black is "due" on the next spin. In reality, each spin is independent, and the probability remains unchanged.
- **Stock markets:** Investors may assume that a stock that has fallen for several days is "due" for a rebound, ignoring that price movements often follow complex, independent, or stochastic processes.
- **Sports outcomes:** Fans may believe a team on a winning streak is "likely" to lose next, despite each game being independent and influenced by numerous factors.

The gambler's fallacy reflects a misunderstanding of randomness: the mistaken belief that events must "even out" in the short term, when in fact probability is only meaningful over large numbers of trials.

The Clustering Illusion

Closely related is the clustering illusion, the tendency to perceive patterns or streaks in random data, even when no meaningful structure exists. Humans are prone to seeing clusters as evidence of causality or design, rather than as expected occurrences in a random process.

Examples:

- **Financial markets:** Traders may interpret a cluster of gains or losses as a trend, overestimating predictability and ignoring statistical noise.
- **Gambling:** Slot machine players perceive streaks of wins or losses, attributing them to skill or luck, when they are natural variations in random sequences.
- **Everyday life:** Noticing coincidences for example, meeting multiple old friends in one week can create the illusion of unusual patterns, even though they occur at rates consistent with chance.

Clusters are not evidence of underlying patterns; they are intrinsic to randomness. Understanding this helps prevent overreaction to short-term sequences and reduces unnecessary risk-taking.

Why These Biases Matter in Decision-Making

Both the gambler's fallacy and clustering illusion interfere with probabilistic thinking:

- They distort perception of risk and reward by creating false expectations of balance or predictability.
- They encourage reactive decisions based on perceived patterns rather than statistical reality.
- They undermine long-term planning by focusing attention on short-term randomness rather than expected value or base rates.

Strategies to Mitigate These Biases

- **Recognize independence:** Understand that many events are statistically independent; past outcomes do not influence future results.
- **Focus on long-term probabilities:** Avoid drawing conclusions from small sample sizes; randomness evens out over large numbers of trials.
- **Quantify expectations:** Use base rates, probability distributions, and expected value to guide decisions rather than relying on perceived patterns.

- **Question patterns:** When noticing streaks or clusters, ask whether they could reasonably arise from random variation.
- **Stress-test assumptions:** Apply scenario analysis to examine how decisions would perform under true randomness.

By understanding the gambler's fallacy and clustering illusion, we begin to see randomness as it truly is: inherently unpredictable, often streaky, and full of apparent patterns that are purely coincidental. Recognizing these biases allows us to resist the temptation to infer false causality, make more rational probabilistic assessments, and avoid unnecessary risk-taking based on misleading impressions.

5.3 Loss Aversion & Probability Neglect

Even when we understand randomness and expected value, human emotion can skew our perception of risk. Two powerful biases *loss aversion* and *probability neglect* consistently distort decision-making under uncertainty. Together, they explain why people often make choices that are emotionally satisfying in the short term but suboptimal in the long term.

Loss Aversion

Loss aversion is the psychological phenomenon whereby the pain of losing is felt more intensely than the pleasure of an equivalent gain. In other words, a loss of \$100 often feels more consequential than a gain of \$100. This asymmetry in perception of outcomes drives behavior that is overly cautious, reactive, and sometimes irrational.

Examples of Loss Aversion:

- **Investing:** Investors may hold losing positions for too long, hoping to avoid realizing a loss, or sell winning positions too early to "lock in gains."
- **Business decisions:** Companies may reject profitable innovations because of fear of potential downside or short-term losses.
- **Personal choices:** People often avoid opportunities with small chances of failure, even if the expected value of the opportunity is positive.

Loss aversion explains why humans are more sensitive to negative outcomes than positive ones, often resulting in decisions that reduce long-term expected value.

Probability Neglect

Probability neglect occurs when people focus on the severity of an outcome rather than its likelihood. Rare but dramatic events receive disproportionate attention, while more probable, less sensational events are ignored.

Examples of Probability Neglect:

- **Insurance:** Individuals may over-insure against highly improbable disasters, like plane crashes, while neglecting common risks such as car accidents.
- **Media influence:** News coverage often exaggerates rare events, such as shark attacks or terrorist incidents, leading the public to overestimate their probability.
- **Gambling and lotteries:** People may chase extremely unlikely jackpots while ignoring bets with better expected value.

Probability neglect interacts with loss aversion: we are drawn to avoid severe losses, even when the chance of their occurrence is minuscule, distorting our assessment of rational risk.

Implications for Decision-Making

Both biases influence behavior in ways that undermine probabilistic reasoning:

- **Overweighting rare events:** People exaggerate the importance of extreme outcomes while underestimating likely ones.
- **Avoiding high-expected-value opportunities:** Fear of small losses can prevent participation in decisions that are advantageous over time.
- **Mispricing risk:** Emotional responses can lead to misjudged risks, resulting in either excessive caution or reckless behavior.

These biases are particularly dangerous because they operate subconsciously, making even experienced decision-makers vulnerable to misjudgments in finance, business, and personal life.

Strategies to Mitigate Loss Aversion and Probability Neglect

- **Quantify probabilities and outcomes:** Replace subjective feelings with objective estimates wherever possible.
- **Use expected value calculations:** Compare potential gains and losses probabilistically, rather than emotionally.

- **Focus on long-term compounding:** Recognize that occasional losses are part of a broader strategy when expected value is positive.
- **Predefine risk tolerance:** Establish limits and stop-loss rules to reduce emotional decision-making under uncertainty.
- **Perspective-taking:** Consider how small, unlikely risks compare to more probable outcomes to correct distorted perception.

In summary, loss aversion and probability neglect are powerful psychological forces that bias our evaluation of risk and probability. By acknowledging these tendencies and applying structured, probabilistic frameworks, we can align decisions with expected value, avoid emotional traps, and make rational choices even in the face of uncertainty. Mastery over these biases is essential for developing a disciplined, probabilistic mindset that thrives in complex and uncertain environments.

Part II

Building the Probabilistic Mindset

Chapter 6

Thinking in Distributions, Not Points

When making decisions under uncertainty, most people instinctively think in absolutes: one predicted outcome, one "most likely" number, or a single-point forecast. This approach, while comforting, ignores the inherent variability of reality. Life, markets, and human behavior rarely conform to exact predictions.

This chapter introduces the concept of thinking in distributions rather than points. By considering a range of possible outcomes and their associated probabilities, you gain a more accurate, nuanced, and actionable understanding of risk and opportunity. Embracing this mindset allows you to account for variance, avoid overconfidence, and make decisions that are robust across a spectrum of possibilities.

We will explore how to visualize outcomes as probability curves, interpret ranges rather than single numbers, and integrate uncertainty into your decision-making process. By the end of this chapter, you will understand why a probabilistic mindset is incomplete without the ability to think in distributions.

6.1 Moving Beyond Single-Point Predictions

Human intuition craves certainty. When faced with complex decisions, we often gravitate toward a single "most likely" outcome a point estimate that simplifies our thinking and provides the illusion of control. While single-point predictions are easier to communicate and understand, they are inherently misleading. They ignore the full spectrum of possibilities and leave decision-makers vulnerable to unexpected outcomes.

The Limitation of Point Estimates

Point predictions are most commonly used in everyday life and professional contexts:

- Forecasting stock prices, revenue, or project completion dates.
- Estimating time to reach personal or career goals.
- Predicting the outcome of sports, elections, or business initiatives.

The problem is that these predictions imply precision that does not exist. Life is rarely linear, and events are influenced by a multitude of interacting variables, many of which are unknown or inherently unpredictable. A single-point forecast conveys a false sense of certainty and often underestimates the likelihood of extreme outcomes, both positive and negative.

The Advantages of Thinking in Ranges

Instead of committing to one value, thinking in ranges acknowledges uncertainty and captures the probabilistic nature of the world. For example:

- Rather than predicting a stock will close at $100, consider it has a 50% chance of being between $95–$105, a 30% chance of $90–$95, and a 20% chance of $105–$120.
- Instead of claiming a project will take exactly 30 days, identify a range: 25–35 days with 70% confidence, 20–40 days with 90% confidence.

By framing predictions in ranges, you account for variance, avoid overconfidence, and create a more resilient decision-making framework. Ranges make it easier to prepare for contingencies and design strategies that are robust under different scenarios.

Applications in Real Life and Business

- **Finance:** Portfolio managers rarely rely on a single expected return; they evaluate distributions of returns to manage risk and allocate capital efficiently.
- **Project Management:** Gantt charts and probabilistic scheduling tools incorporate uncertainty by using ranges for task durations rather than fixed deadlines.
- **Entrepreneurship:** Startups assess potential revenue or customer growth not as a single figure but across a range of plausible outcomes, accounting for market volatility and operational risks.

- **Personal Decisions:** Career planning, health outcomes, or life goals benefit from range-based thinking, which reduces the psychological stress of uncertainty and highlights alternative strategies.

Key Takeaways

- Single-point predictions are comforting but often misleading.
- Thinking in ranges acknowledges uncertainty and improves probabilistic decision-making.
- Range-based thinking enhances risk management, scenario planning, and strategic flexibility.
- Moving beyond point predictions is essential to develop a robust probabilistic mindset.

In short, replacing single-point predictions with distributions or ranges transforms how we approach uncertainty. It forces us to consider multiple outcomes, anticipate variability, and prepare for the unexpected, turning probabilistic thinking from a theoretical concept into a practical tool for smarter decision-making.

6.2 Ranges and Probability Curves

Once we move beyond single-point predictions, the next step in probabilistic thinking is to visualize outcomes as ranges and probability distributions. Ranges provide simple bounds, while probability curves offer a richer understanding of how likely each outcome is within those bounds. Together, they transform abstract uncertainty into actionable insight.

Understanding Ranges

Ranges are a straightforward way to represent uncertainty. Instead of predicting that an event will take exactly one value, we specify a low, most likely, and high estimate. For example:

- A project might take 25–35 days, with 30 days being the most likely.
- A startup's revenue might fall between $500,000 and $1,000,000 next year, with a midpoint of $750,000.

Ranges communicate variability and encourage planning for best-case, worst-case, and most probable scenarios. They also counteract overconfidence by explicitly showing the uncertainty around the estimate.

From Ranges to Probability Curves

While ranges are useful, they do not capture the probability of different outcomes within the range. Probability curves, or probability density functions, do. They allow us to assign weights to different potential outcomes:

- **Uniform distribution:** Every value within the range is equally likely.
- **Normal distribution:** Outcomes near the mean are more likely, and extremes are less probable.
- **Skewed distribution:** Certain outcomes have higher likelihood, reflecting asymmetry or biased risks.

Visualizing a probability curve helps us understand not only the range of possibilities but also where most outcomes are concentrated. This is crucial for decision-making under uncertainty because it highlights the most probable scenarios while accounting for rare but impactful events.

Applications and Examples

- **Finance:** Traders use probability curves to model expected returns and potential losses, assessing the likelihood of extreme market movements.
- **Project Management:** Monte Carlo simulations generate thousands of possible project timelines, producing a probability distribution that informs realistic deadlines and contingency planning.
- **Entrepreneurship:** Startups model revenue or user growth using probability distributions, helping investors and founders understand upside potential and downside risk.
- **Everyday Life:** Even personal decisions like estimating travel time or planning savings goals benefit from visualizing ranges and likelihoods rather than relying on a single expected number.

Why Probability Curves Matter

- They reveal the concentration of probable outcomes, enabling better risk assessment.
- They highlight tail risks low-probability but high-impact events so you can plan for them.
- They improve decision-making by allowing trade-offs between likely scenarios and extreme events.

- They enhance communication, providing a clearer picture of uncertainty to stakeholders, colleagues, or collaborators.

Key Takeaways

- Ranges provide a first step toward acknowledging uncertainty; probability curves refine that understanding by assigning likelihoods to outcomes.
- Visualizing distributions reduces overconfidence, highlights tail risks, and supports more informed decisions.
- Incorporating probability curves into your thinking transforms abstract uncertainty into practical guidance for action.

By thinking in probability curves rather than single points, you embrace the full complexity of uncertainty. You gain the ability to see where outcomes are most likely, recognize rare but consequential possibilities, and make decisions that are resilient across a spectrum of futures. This approach is central to building a truly probabilistic mindset.

6.3 Embracing Variance in Outcomes

Variance the natural spread of possible outcomes is one of the most powerful yet underappreciated concepts in probabilistic thinking. Life rarely unfolds exactly as expected. Projects take longer or shorter than planned, markets swing unpredictably, and personal decisions yield results that deviate from our initial predictions. Embracing variance means recognizing that uncertainty is inherent in every decision, and that outcomes exist along a spectrum rather than a single point.

Why Variance Matters

Variance is central to understanding risk and probability. It quantifies the degree of deviation around an expected outcome. A low-variance situation has outcomes tightly clustered around a mean, while high variance indicates wide dispersion, with outcomes ranging from extremely negative to extraordinarily positive. Ignoring variance leads to overconfidence, poor risk management, and an inability to anticipate extreme scenarios.

Understanding variance allows you to:

- Assess potential upside and downside realistically.
- Prepare for unlikely but high-impact events.

- Make decisions that remain robust across a wide range of possible outcomes.
- Reduce emotional stress by framing unexpected results as normal rather than catastrophic.

Real-World Examples of Variance

- **Investing:** Stocks, cryptocurrencies, and venture capital investments exhibit high variance. Some investments may fail completely, while others generate enormous returns. Understanding this helps investors construct portfolios that balance potential rewards with manageable risk.
- **Entrepreneurship:** Most startups fail, but a few achieve outsized success. Entrepreneurs who embrace variance make small, experimental bets and diversify their efforts, allowing them to capture high upside without catastrophic exposure.
- **Career Choices:** Pursuing high-variance paths such as creative endeavors or leadership roles in emerging industries can produce extraordinary career outcomes, but also carries a wide spectrum of potential setbacks. Planning for variance reduces stress and improves long-term career strategy.
- **Everyday Life:** Even mundane decisions, such as travel time, health outcomes, or personal projects, are subject to variance. Accounting for it improves planning, reduces disappointment, and fosters flexibility.

Strategies to Embrace Variance

- **Scenario Planning:** Consider multiple outcomes best-case, worst-case, and most probable and prepare strategies for each scenario.
- **Optionality:** Structure decisions so that you can capitalize on favorable outcomes while limiting losses if the worst-case scenario occurs.
- **Probabilistic Decision-Making:** Shift focus from deterministic goals to probabilistic expectations. Make choices that maximize expected value across a distribution of outcomes, not just for a single predicted point.
- **Iterative Learning:** Treat outcomes as feedback. High variance environments provide rapid learning opportunities; adapt your decisions as new data emerges.

- **Psychological Preparation:** Recognize that wide outcome distributions are normal. Reducing fear of negative extremes enhances emotional resilience and prevents impulsive reactions.

Psychological Benefits of Embracing Variance

Resisting variance often stems from a desire for certainty and control. By embracing it:

- You develop mental flexibility and reduce stress from unexpected results.
- You cultivate patience and resilience, understanding that short-term deviations are part of a long-term trajectory.
- You enhance your ability to take calculated risks without succumbing to fear or overconfidence.
- You begin to see surprises not as failures but as opportunities for learning and growth.

Key Takeaways

- Variance is an inherent feature of uncertainty, not a flaw to be avoided.
- Recognizing and planning for variance strengthens decision-making and risk management.
- Embracing variance fosters psychological resilience and reduces overreaction to unexpected outcomes.
- Decisions that account for variance are more robust, flexible, and aligned with a probabilistic mindset.
- Mastery of variance allows you to convert uncertainty into a competitive edge, enabling smarter decisions across life, business, and finance.

Ultimately, embracing variance transforms how you interact with uncertainty. Instead of fearing unpredictability, you recognize it as a fundamental aspect of reality. This perspective allows you to navigate life with foresight, resilience, and a clear-eyed understanding that outcomes are distributions rather than fixed points,

Chapter 7

Scenario Planning Alternative Futures

Life rarely unfolds according to a single plan. Unforeseen events, shifting circumstances, and hidden variables can dramatically alter the outcomes of even the most carefully laid strategies. This is where scenario planning and the consideration of alternative futures become essential tools for the probabilistic thinker.

Rather than predicting a single outcome, scenario planning encourages us to develop multiple plausible futures, each grounded in a set of assumptions. By exploring "what if" pathways and stress-testing decisions across different scenarios, we prepare for uncertainty, identify risks, and uncover opportunities that might otherwise remain hidden.

In this chapter, we will examine how to formulate multiple hypotheses about the future, design decision pathways that are robust across various outcomes, and stress-test your strategies to ensure resilience under uncertainty. By the end, you will understand how thinking in scenarios transforms reactive decision-making into proactive, probabilistic strategy.

7.1 The Value of Multiple Hypotheses

One of the most powerful tools in probabilistic thinking is the ability to generate and evaluate multiple hypotheses about the future. Relying on a single hypothesis "this will happen" is a form of deterministic thinking that leaves decision-makers vulnerable to surprises. In contrast, considering multiple plausible futures allows us to anticipate uncertainty, identify potential risks and opportunities, and make more robust decisions.

Why a Single Hypothesis Fails

Relying on a single prediction assumes that the world behaves in a linear, predictable manner. This is rarely the case. Complex systems financial markets, organizational dynamics, geopolitical developments, and even personal life events are influenced by numerous interacting variables. A single hypothesis often:

- Overlooks alternative possibilities that may dramatically impact outcomes.
- Increases overconfidence, leading to excessive risk-taking or under preparation.
- Fails to account for low-probability, high-impact events, commonly known as "tail risks."

Generating Multiple Hypotheses

Creating multiple hypotheses involves systematically imagining different ways the future might unfold. Techniques include:

- **Brainstorming extremes:** Consider best-case, worst-case, and most likely scenarios.
- **Historical analogues:** Examine similar events or situations in the past and extrapolate plausible outcomes.
- **Red teaming:** Challenge your assumptions by deliberately looking for weaknesses or alternative perspectives.
- **Counterfactual thinking:** Ask "what if" questions that explore how small changes could lead to significantly different results.

By generating multiple hypotheses, we reduce the risk of surprise and enhance our ability to respond adaptively as events unfold.

Applications in Decision-Making

- **Investing:** Instead of assuming a single market trend, investors consider multiple market scenarios bullish, bearish, and sideways and design portfolios that are resilient across them.
- **Business strategy:** Companies use scenario planning to anticipate regulatory changes, technological disruptions, or shifts in consumer behavior, allowing them to pivot quickly.

- **Personal life:** Career planning, relocation, or major purchases benefit from imagining multiple possible futures, such as changes in job market conditions or personal circumstances.

Benefits of Multiple Hypotheses

- **Reduces overconfidence:** Considering alternative outcomes keeps assumptions in check.
- **Enhances flexibility:** Multiple hypotheses provide options when reality diverges from expectations.
- **Improves risk management:** By anticipating a range of outcomes, you can allocate resources and implement strategies that mitigate downside while preserving upside.
- **Supports probabilistic thinking:** Each hypothesis can be assigned a probability, allowing decision-making to be guided by expected value rather than intuition alone.

Key Takeaways

- Relying on a single hypothesis exposes you to unnecessary risk and surprise.
- Generating multiple plausible futures strengthens resilience and adaptability.
- Systematic exploration of different scenarios enables better risk assessment, planning, and decision-making.
- The value of multiple hypotheses lies in its ability to transform uncertainty from a threat into a source of strategic advantage.

In essence, thinking in multiple hypotheses is a cornerstone of probabilistic reasoning. It shifts the mindset from predicting a single outcome to preparing for a spectrum of possibilities, making your decisions more robust, adaptive, and ultimately more likely to succeed in an uncertain world.

7.2 Designing "What If" Pathways

Once multiple hypotheses about the future are established, the next critical step is designing "what if" pathways. These pathways map out potential sequences of events, decisions, and consequences for each scenario, allowing you to explore the ripple effects of uncertainty. Unlike single-point forecasts, which imply a linear trajectory, "what if" pathways embrace complexity, showing how one choice or external event can cascade into multiple outcomes.

The Purpose of "What If" Pathways

"What if" pathways serve several purposes in probabilistic decision-making:

- **Visualizing complexity:** They help you see how interconnected factors interact and influence outcomes.
- **Anticipating consequences:** By mapping different possibilities, you identify potential risks, bottlenecks, and opportunities.
- **Supporting proactive strategy:** Pathways guide the development of contingency plans, rather than reactive responses to surprises.
- **Encouraging flexible thinking:** They prevent rigid adherence to a single plan by showing multiple avenues and outcomes.

Steps to Design "What If" Pathways

Start with hypotheses: Use the multiple plausible scenarios you've generated as starting points. **Identify key drivers:** Determine the critical variables that will influence outcomes in each scenario. This could include market trends, regulatory changes, technology shifts, or personal decisions. **Map branching outcomes:** For each key driver, explore how different actions or events could lead to divergent results. Consider best-case, worst-case, and intermediate possibilities. **Assign probabilities (optional):** Where possible, attach probabilities to each branch, transforming qualitative pathways into quantitative, decision-guiding tools. **Evaluate implications:** Identify which pathways carry the highest risks or greatest opportunities, and determine how to prepare or respond accordingly.

Applications in Decision-Making

- **Business Strategy:** Companies often simulate scenarios such as market disruption, regulatory change, or competitive innovation. Each pathway outlines potential strategic responses and outcomes, helping leaders make informed decisions.
- **Investing:** Investors can model how changes in interest rates, economic cycles, or geopolitical events may affect portfolio performance, creating pathways that anticipate losses and capitalize on upside opportunities.

- **Project Management:** Project managers can identify bottlenecks, dependencies, and risk points by mapping out alternative execution pathways, allowing for better resource allocation and scheduling.
- **Personal Life:** From career moves to financial planning, individuals can use "what if" pathways to visualize consequences of different choices, improving preparedness and reducing regret.

Benefits of "What If" Pathways

- **Reduces surprises:** By exploring multiple outcomes, you are less likely to be caught off guard by unexpected events.
- **Improves risk management:** Pathways highlight potential pitfalls and tail risks, enabling you to hedge against downside while preserving upside.
- **Enhances strategic flexibility:** Multiple pathways provide alternative options when reality deviates from expectations.
- **Supports probabilistic thinking:** Pathways integrate both qualitative and quantitative analysis, enhancing decision quality in complex and uncertain environments.

Key Takeaways

- "What if" pathways turn abstract scenarios into actionable insights.
- They map the consequences of key variables and decisions, revealing interconnections and potential outcomes.
- Designing these pathways reduces overconfidence, strengthens planning, and fosters flexible, adaptive thinking.
- When combined with multiple hypotheses, "what if" pathways provide a robust framework for navigating uncertainty and making decisions that are resilient across a range of futures.

In short, designing "what if" pathways transforms scenario planning from a theoretical exercise into a practical tool for probabilistic decision-making. By systematically mapping how different choices and events could unfold, you equip yourself to respond proactively, capitalize on opportunities, and mitigate risks in an uncertain world.

7.3 Stress-Testing Decisions

After generating multiple hypotheses and designing "what if" pathways, the final step in robust scenario planning is stress-testing your decisions. Stress-testing involves deliberately examining how your plans perform under extreme, unexpected, or adverse conditions. The goal is not to predict every possible outcome, but to understand vulnerabilities, anticipate risks, and identify areas where your strategies may fail or require adaptation.

Why Stress-Testing Matters

Decisions made without stress-testing assume that the world will behave as expected. In reality, even well-researched plans can fail due to rare but impactful events, unforeseen dependencies, or human error. Stress-testing provides insight into:

- **Tail risks:** Low-probability but high-impact events that could dramatically alter outcomes.
- **System weaknesses:** Areas where assumptions or strategies are fragile and prone to failure.
- **Decision resilience:** How robust your plan is across a variety of scenarios and contingencies.

Stress-testing transforms uncertainty from a source of anxiety into actionable knowledge. By identifying potential failure points in advance, you can create contingencies, hedge risks, and increase the probability of long-term success.

Methods for Stress-Testing Decisions

- **Scenario simulation:** Test your plan against extreme outcomes or unlikely but plausible scenarios. For example, a startup could examine the impact of losing a key investor or facing a sudden market downturn.
- **Sensitivity analysis:** Evaluate how changes in critical variables affect outcomes. This helps identify which assumptions have the greatest impact on results.
- **Red-teaming:** Assign a team or an individual to challenge assumptions, expose blind spots, and explore ways the plan could fail.
- **Reverse stress-testing:** Start with the worst-case outcome and work backward to determine what events or failures could lead to it, then design mitigations.

- **Probabilistic evaluation:** Assign probabilities to adverse events and assess their impact on your expected outcomes, ensuring your decisions remain robust under uncertainty.

Applications Across Domains

- **Finance:** Investors stress-test portfolios against extreme market scenarios, interest rate shocks, or geopolitical events to avoid catastrophic losses.
- **Business:** Companies examine supply chain disruptions, regulatory changes, or technological failures to ensure operational resilience.
- **Project Management:** Teams evaluate how resource shortages, scheduling delays, or technical failures could impact deadlines and deliverables.
- **Personal Life:** Individuals stress-test career, financial, or health plans by considering unexpected events such as job loss, economic downturns, or sudden expenses.

Benefits of Stress-Testing

- **Reduces vulnerability:** Identifies weaknesses before they cause real damage.
- **Enhances adaptability:** Prepares you to pivot quickly when reality deviates from expectations.
- **Improves decision confidence:** Knowing that a plan has been rigorously tested increases psychological resilience.
- **Supports probabilistic thinking:** Emphasizes that outcomes exist on a spectrum and that preparation for low-probability events is essential.

Key Takeaways

- Stress-testing is an essential step in scenario planning, revealing vulnerabilities and tail risks.
- It enables proactive mitigation of risks and enhances resilience across multiple scenarios.
- Combining stress-testing with multiple hypotheses and "what if" pathways creates a robust framework for navigating uncertainty.

- Regularly revisiting and updating stress-tests ensures that decisions remain adaptive in dynamic environments.

In essence, stress-testing transforms theoretical scenarios into actionable insights. It bridges the gap between probabilistic thinking and real-world decision-making, ensuring that your strategies are not only well-informed but also resilient to the unexpected. By stress-testing your plans, you prepare yourself to thrive in an uncertain world rather than merely survive it.

Chapter 8

Decision-Making Under Uncertainty

Every decision we make occurs under uncertainty. Rarely do we have perfect information, and the outcomes of our choices are shaped by factors beyond our control. In such an environment, relying solely on intuition or deterministic reasoning can be costly.

Decision-making under uncertainty requires a structured approach that incorporates new information as it becomes available, reduces cognitive biases, and balances analytical reasoning with human intuition. By adopting probabilistic frameworks, you can evaluate options more objectively, update your beliefs dynamically, and make choices that are resilient across a range of possible outcomes.

In this chapter, we explore three essential tools for decision-making under uncertainty: Bayesian updating for dynamically refining beliefs, checklists to ensure comprehensive probabilistic reasoning, and strategies for balancing intuition with analytical rigor. Together, these tools provide a roadmap for making smarter, more adaptive decisions in a complex and unpredictable world.

8.1 Bayesian Updating

At the heart of probabilistic decision-making lies the principle of updating your beliefs as new information becomes available. This principle, formalized in Bayesian statistics, allows us to revise our expectations systematically and make decisions that are continuously informed by evidence. Bayesian updating is not merely a mathematical formula it is a mindset that transforms uncertainty into actionable insight.

The Core Idea

Bayesian updating is based on the concept that your initial beliefs about the world your *prior probabilities* are provisional and should be adjusted when new data arrives. The revised belief, known as the *posterior probability*, combines your prior knowledge with the likelihood of the observed evidence. In simple terms, Bayesian updating asks:

> "Given what I previously believed, and the new information I just observed, what should I now believe?"

Why It Matters in Decision-Making

Without updating beliefs, we risk making decisions based on outdated or incomplete information. In real-world environments:

- Conditions change constantly markets fluctuate, technologies evolve, and competitors adapt.
- Data is often noisy, uncertain, or partial, requiring careful interpretation.
- Cognitive biases, such as confirmation bias, can prevent us from properly integrating new evidence.

Bayesian updating provides a structured framework to incorporate new evidence objectively, improving decision quality over time.

Practical Example

Imagine you are considering investing in a startup. Based on prior experience, you estimate a 30% chance that the startup will succeed. Then you learn that the founding team has successfully launched two previous ventures. This new information increases the likelihood of success. Using Bayesian thinking, you revise your estimate upward, perhaps to 45–50%, reflecting both your prior belief and the new evidence. Each subsequent data point market trends, customer traction, or financial performance further refines your probability estimate.

Steps to Apply Bayesian Updating in Everyday Decisions

1. **Identify your prior:** Establish your initial belief about an outcome based on experience, historical data, or intuition.
2. **Collect new evidence:** Gather relevant information that can inform or challenge your prior belief.

3. **Assess likelihoods:** Determine how probable the new evidence is under different possible outcomes.

4. **Update beliefs:** Adjust your initial probability based on how strongly the new evidence supports or contradicts it.

5. **Repeat iteratively:** As new information arrives, continue to revise your beliefs, improving decision quality over time.

Applications Across Domains

- **Investing:** Continuously update market expectations and portfolio decisions based on financial news, earnings reports, and macroeconomic data.
- **Entrepreneurship:** Adjust assumptions about product-market fit, customer demand, or growth potential as new metrics and feedback arrive.
- **Medical Decisions:** Doctors use Bayesian reasoning to refine diagnoses as test results and symptoms accumulate.
- **Personal Life:** Bayesian updating can guide career choices, relationship decisions, or lifestyle changes by integrating new experiences and outcomes.

Psychological and Strategic Benefits

- **Reduces overconfidence:** Continuously updating beliefs keeps assumptions in check.
- **Enhances adaptability:** Decisions evolve as reality changes, rather than being rigidly fixed.
- **Improves probabilistic reasoning:** Integrating evidence systematically fosters a more accurate understanding of uncertainty.
- **Supports learning and compounding:** Each update refines your mental model, allowing small advantages to accumulate into substantial long-term insight.

Key Takeaways

- Bayesian updating is a structured framework for revising beliefs based on new evidence.
- It transforms uncertainty from a liability into a dynamic source of information.
- Applying Bayesian principles improves decision-making across finance, business, medicine, and everyday life.
- Mastering Bayesian updating cultivates mental flexibility, resilience, and a probabilistic edge in a world defined by uncertainty.

In essence, Bayesian updating is a mindset as much as a technique. By continuously integrating new information and adjusting your beliefs, you shift from rigid, deterministic thinking to a fluid, probabilistic approach that allows you to navigate uncertainty with clarity, confidence, and strategic foresight.

8.2 Checklists for Probabilistic Decisions

Even the most experienced decision-makers are prone to errors when navigating uncertainty. Cognitive biases, emotional reactions, and overlooked variables can all lead to flawed judgments. One of the most effective tools for mitigating these risks is the use of checklists tailored for probabilistic decision-making. A checklist is not a rigid formula; rather, it is a structured guide that ensures critical factors are considered, assumptions are challenged, and probability-driven reasoning is consistently applied.

Why Checklists Work

Checklists succeed where intuition alone often fails because they:

- **Reduce cognitive load:** By providing a structured framework, checklists help prevent oversight and mental fatigue.
- **Counteract biases:** Systematic prompts can expose overconfidence, hindsight bias, and probability neglect.
- **Promote consistency:** Using checklists ensures that decisions are evaluated using the same rigorous criteria each time.
- **Encourage probabilistic thinking:** Checklists remind decision-makers to consider ranges, distributions, and likelihoods rather than single-point predictions.

Core Components of a Probabilistic Decision Checklist

A checklist for probabilistic decisions should cover multiple dimensions:

1. **Define the decision clearly:** What exactly is being decided, and what is the time horizon for outcomes?
2. **Identify assumptions:** List explicit and implicit assumptions. Are they based on reliable data or intuition?
3. **Evaluate probabilities:** Assign probabilities to potential outcomes and consider their ranges, not just the most likely scenario.
4. **Assess variance and tail risks:** Identify high-impact, low-probability events that could influence results.
5. **Consider alternatives:** Explore multiple hypotheses and "what if" pathways.
6. **Analyze expected value:** Calculate or estimate the expected value of each option, accounting for both upside and downside.
7. **Check for biases:** Actively search for overconfidence, confirmation bias, anchoring, or emotional influences.
8. **Plan contingencies:** Determine how you would respond if outcomes deviate significantly from expectations.
9. **Document the decision process:** Record your reasoning and assumptions to facilitate learning and future updates.

Applications of Checklists

- **Investing:** Investors can use checklists to evaluate potential trades, ensuring all risks, probabilities, and edge calculations are considered.
- **Entrepreneurship:** Founders can systematically assess new ventures, product launches, or strategic pivots.
- **Project Management:** Teams can evaluate project plans, resource allocations, and risk mitigation strategies using structured prompts.
- **Personal Decisions:** Career moves, large purchases, or relocation decisions benefit from a checklist that incorporates probabilistic thinking and scenario analysis.

Psychological and Strategic Benefits

- **Reduces errors under pressure:** Checklists prevent impulsive or emotionally-driven decisions.
- **Enhances learning:** Documenting the process allows reflection and iterative improvement over time.
- **Increases confidence:** Knowing that decisions are systematically evaluated increases clarity and reduces regret.
- **Supports probabilistic literacy:** Regular use reinforces a mindset focused on likelihoods, expected value, and distributions rather than certainty.

Key Takeaways

- Checklists are a practical tool for applying probabilistic thinking in real-world decisions.
- They mitigate cognitive biases, reduce oversight, and ensure that critical variables and assumptions are considered.
- Effective checklists integrate probabilities, variance, tail risks, alternative hypotheses, and contingency planning.
- Regular use cultivates discipline, strategic clarity, and a mental edge in navigating uncertainty.

By incorporating checklists into your decision-making process, you create a structured framework that transforms uncertainty from a source of anxiety into a tool for informed action. They bridge the gap between probabilistic theory and everyday practice, ensuring that each choice is carefully evaluated, resilient to surprises, and aligned with long-term goals.

8.3 Balancing Intuition and Analysis

Decision-making under uncertainty is a delicate dance between intuition and analytical reasoning. While probabilistic frameworks, Bayesian updating, and checklists provide structure, human intuition remains an invaluable guide, especially in situations where data is limited or ambiguous. The key is learning when to trust intuition, when to rely on analysis, and how to integrate both for optimal decision outcomes.

The Role of Intuition

Intuition is the brain's ability to recognize patterns, draw on accumulated experience, and make rapid judgments without conscious deliberation. It is particularly useful when:

- **Information is incomplete:** Decisions must be made quickly with limited data.
- **Time is constrained:** Immediate responses are required, such as in negotiations or crisis situations.
- **Experience is relevant:** Past exposure to similar patterns allows subconscious recognition of likely outcomes.

However, intuition is prone to biases, overconfidence, and errors in complex or unfamiliar environments. Without analytical checks, it can lead to systematically poor decisions.

The Role of Analysis

Analytical reasoning complements intuition by providing:

- **Structured evaluation:** Systematic frameworks like Bayesian updating, expected value calculations, and scenario analysis.
- **Quantitative insights:** Use of probability distributions, variance, and metrics to guide decisions.
- **Bias mitigation:** Analytical processes challenge intuitive assumptions and reduce overconfidence.

Analysis, however, can become paralyzing if taken to extremes. Excessive deliberation, data overload, or false precision can stall decisions, especially when timely action is critical.

Integrating Intuition and Analysis

The goal is not to choose between intuition and analysis, but to blend them effectively:

1. **Use intuition as a hypothesis generator:** Let gut instincts suggest potential options or solutions.
2. **Validate with analysis:** Apply probabilistic reasoning, checklists, and scenario evaluation to test intuitive judgments.

3. **Iterate dynamically:** Allow analytical insights to refine intuition, and let intuitive pattern recognition guide focus where data is sparse or noisy.

4. **Know domain limits:** Rely on intuition in areas where experience is rich, but default to analysis in novel or high-stakes situations.

Practical Applications

- **Investing:** An experienced trader's intuition may highlight emerging trends, which are then validated through probabilistic risk assessment and portfolio analytics.

- **Entrepreneurship:** A founder's instinct about product-market fit can guide early strategy, while market research and scenario modeling provide quantitative support.

- **Negotiation:** Intuition helps read the room and sense leverage, while game-theoretic analysis informs optimal concessions and offers.

- **Personal Life:** Career or relationship decisions benefit from intuition shaped by personal values, combined with logical evaluation of probabilities, potential outcomes, and trade-offs.

Benefits of Balancing Intuition and Analysis

- **Enhanced decision quality:** Leveraging both human pattern recognition and structured reasoning produces more robust outcomes.

- **Reduced bias:** Analysis checks intuitive errors, while intuition prevents over-reliance on incomplete or noisy data.

- **Faster yet informed decisions:** Intuition accelerates judgment, while analysis ensures rigor.

- **Adaptive learning:** Continuous interplay between intuition and analysis strengthens both faculties over time.

Key Takeaways

- Neither intuition nor analysis alone is sufficient for navigating uncertainty.

- Intuition excels in rapid, experience-based judgments; analysis provides structure, objectivity, and probability-based rigor.

- Integrating the two enables faster, more accurate, and resilient decision-making.
- Mastery comes from iterative practice: using intuition to guide hypotheses, and analysis to validate, refine, and stress-test those instincts.

In essence, balancing intuition and analysis transforms uncertainty from a source of anxiety into a navigable landscape. By learning when to trust your instincts and when to defer to structured reasoning, you gain the flexibility, clarity, and confidence to make smarter decisions in complex, probabilistic environments.

Chapter 9

Mental Models for Probabilistic Thinking

The human mind naturally gravitates toward linear thinking cause leads to effect, action produces a predictable result. But in complex, uncertain environments, linearity is rare. Outcomes are shaped by interacting variables, feedback loops, and probabilistic events. To navigate such complexity, we rely on mental models frameworks that simplify reality and help us reason more effectively.

In this chapter, we explore three powerful mental models specifically tailored for probabilistic thinking. *Inversion* teaches us to think backwards from failure to success, uncovering hidden pitfalls. *Second-order thinking* pushes us to consider the consequences of consequences, moving beyond superficial analysis. And the *Kelly Criterion and edge-based frameworks* provide a mathematical foundation for allocating resources where probabilities and potential payoffs intersect optimally. Together, these models give you a structured toolkit to reason clearly, anticipate risks, and leverage uncertainty for advantage.

9.1 Inversion (Thinking Backwards)

Inversion is a mental model that flips conventional thinking on its head: instead of asking, "How do I succeed?" we ask, "How could I fail?" By approaching problems from the perspective of failure, we often uncover hidden risks, blind spots, and overlooked variables that forward-looking thinking might miss. In probabilistic decision-making, inversion is especially powerful because it exposes tail risks, worst-case scenarios, and improbable events that can have outsized consequences.

The Core Idea

The essence of inversion is simple yet profound: rather than solely focusing on the desired outcome, explore its opposite. Consider the question:

> "What actions, decisions, or conditions would make success impossible?"

Once these failure points are identified, you can design strategies to avoid them or mitigate their impact. In other words, by understanding what could go wrong, you increase the probability of things going right.

Why Inversion Matters in Probabilistic Thinking

Forward-looking decision-making often suffers from cognitive biases:

- **Overconfidence:** We assume our plan is sound without examining vulnerabilities.
- **Optimism bias:** We focus on best-case outcomes while underestimating risks.
- **Narrow framing:** We fail to consider rare or extreme events, ignoring "tail risks."

Inversion counteracts these biases by forcing attention to the full spectrum of possible outcomes, especially negative ones. It complements probabilistic tools such as Bayesian updating, expected value, and scenario analysis, providing a mental framework to anticipate problems before they arise.

Practical Applications of Inversion

- **Investing:** Instead of asking, "Which stock will likely rise?" ask, "What could cause this investment to fail?" This highlights risks like market volatility, liquidity issues, or management missteps.
- **Entrepreneurship:** Instead of only envisioning product success, map out reasons why the venture could fail poor timing, competitive response, or flawed execution and develop countermeasures.
- **Negotiation:** Consider what actions or concessions could lead to a failed deal, then structure your approach to avoid those pitfalls.
- **Personal Life:** Career or health decisions benefit from asking, "What could make me fail at this goal?" By addressing these factors proactively, you increase the likelihood of long-term success.

Steps to Apply Inversion

1. **Define the desired outcome:** Be clear about what success looks like.
2. **List potential failure modes:** Brainstorm everything that could prevent success, from common mistakes to improbable catastrophes.
3. **Analyze probabilities:** Estimate the likelihood and impact of each failure mode.
4. **Design mitigations:** Develop strategies to avoid, reduce, or hedge against these failure modes.
5. **Iterate continuously:** As new information emerges, update the failure list and adjust mitigation strategies.

Psychological and Strategic Benefits

- **Reduces blind spots:** Highlights risks that are otherwise ignored in forward-looking thinking.
- **Enhances resilience:** By preparing for potential failures, you can respond effectively when challenges arise.
- **Improves probabilistic reasoning:** Encourages thinking in distributions and likelihoods, rather than assuming deterministic outcomes.
- **Strengthens decision quality:** Avoiding predictable mistakes increases the probability of long-term success.

Key Takeaways

- Inversion flips conventional thinking: focus on what could go wrong instead of only on success.
- It reveals tail risks, hidden dependencies, and failure points often overlooked in forward-looking reasoning.
- Inversion complements probabilistic tools like Bayesian updating, scenario planning, and expected value calculations.
- Regular use cultivates a mindset that anticipates problems, mitigates risks, and increases the likelihood of achieving complex, uncertain goals.

In essence, thinking backwards allows you to see the invisible. By systematically identifying failure points, you not only protect yourself from preventable mistakes but also gain a clearer path toward success. In probabilistic decision-making, inversion transforms uncertainty from a threat into an advantage.

9.2 Second-Order Thinking

Second-order thinking is the mental model that pushes decision-makers to go beyond immediate, obvious consequences and consider the ripple effects the consequences of consequences. While first-order thinking asks, "What will happen if I take this action?" second-order thinking asks, "What happens next, and what are the longer-term implications?" In complex, probabilistic environments, the ability to think in layers significantly improves decision quality and reduces vulnerability to unforeseen outcomes.

The Core Idea

Most decisions are evaluated superficially, focusing only on immediate results. For example, a first-order thinker might invest in a stock simply because its price is rising, ignoring what the rise implies for valuation, market sentiment, or systemic risk. A second-order thinker, however, asks:

> "If I invest in this stock, what chain of events might follow? How will competitors, regulators, or market psychology respond? What hidden risks emerge as a result?"

By systematically considering indirect consequences, you develop a richer understanding of complex systems and can make decisions that are robust to uncertainty.

Why Second-Order Thinking Matters

Second-order thinking is critical because:

- **It uncovers hidden risks:** Many failures occur not from the initial action, but from neglected downstream effects.
- **It reveals hidden opportunities:** Positive second-order effects, like network effects or compounding advantages, can be leveraged strategically.
- **It mitigates overconfidence:** Recognizing the complexity of cause-and-effect chains reduces the tendency to assume simple, deterministic outcomes.
- **It improves probabilistic reasoning:** Understanding multiple layers of consequences allows for more accurate probability assessments and expected value calculations.

Practical Applications of Second-Order Thinking

- **Investing:** Consider not just the direct impact of a company's earnings report, but how it influences market sentiment, regulatory scrutiny, and competitor responses over time.
- **Entrepreneurship:** Evaluate how introducing a new product affects customer behavior, competitor strategies, supply chain dynamics, and long-term brand perception.
- **Policy-making:** Assess how regulations or incentives might produce unintended consequences in other parts of the system.
- **Personal Life:** Anticipate the long-term consequences of career moves, financial choices, or lifestyle changes beyond immediate benefits.

Steps to Apply Second-Order Thinking

1. **Identify the first-order effects:** Understand the immediate and obvious outcomes of a decision.
2. **Trace the second-order consequences:** Ask, "What happens next as a result of this action?" Consider multiple pathways and feedback loops.
3. **Assign probabilities:** Estimate the likelihood of each consequence occurring and its potential impact.
4. **Integrate into decision-making:** Use this layered understanding to weigh options, adjust strategies, and anticipate both risks and opportunities.
5. **Iterate over time:** Re-evaluate consequences as new information arises or the environment changes.

Psychological and Strategic Benefits

- **Reduces shortsightedness:** Encourages thinking beyond immediate gratification or obvious gains.
- **Strengthens foresight:** Anticipates the broader impact of decisions in complex, interconnected systems.
- **Enhances resilience:** Prepares you for unintended consequences, reducing vulnerability to shocks.
- **Improves decision quality:** Promotes a more probabilistic, systemic approach to evaluating choices.

Key Takeaways

- Second-order thinking goes beyond immediate outcomes to evaluate the consequences of consequences.
- It uncovers hidden risks, identifies unexpected opportunities, and strengthens probabilistic reasoning.
- Applying this mental model improves decision-making in investing, entrepreneurship, policy-making, and personal life.
- Regular practice cultivates a habit of anticipating ripple effects, making you a more strategic and resilient thinker.

In essence, second-order thinking allows you to see the hidden layers of cause and effect. By anticipating the chain reactions of your decisions, you move from reactive, first-order choices to strategic, probabilistic decision-making that maximizes long-term outcomes and minimizes unforeseen risks.

9.3 Kelly Criterion & Edge-Based Frameworks

In probabilistic decision-making, understanding not just what to bet on, but how much to bet, can dramatically impact long-term outcomes. The Kelly Criterion, developed by John L. Kelly Jr. in 1956, provides a mathematical framework for optimizing bet size based on probability and payoff. When combined with edge-based thinking focusing on situations where you have a measurable advantage it forms a powerful tool for allocating resources, managing risk, and compounding probabilistic gains over time.

The Core Idea of the Kelly Criterion

The Kelly Criterion answers the question:

> "Given my probability of success and the potential payoff, what fraction of my capital should I allocate to maximize long-term growth while minimizing the risk of ruin?"

Mathematically, for a simple binary outcome, the formula is:

$$f^* = \frac{bp - q}{b}$$

Where:

- f^* = fraction of capital to bet
- b = odds received on the bet (net payoff per unit)

- p = probability of winning
- q = probability of losing (1-p)

The Kelly approach ensures that you never bet too aggressively, which could lead to ruin, nor too conservatively, which reduces growth potential. It balances risk and reward optimally when probabilities and payoffs are known.

Edge-Based Thinking

Edge-based frameworks extend this idea beyond gambling. In any probabilistic environment, an *edge* is a situation where the expected value is positive that is, the odds and potential payoff favor you. The key steps are:

1. Identify scenarios where you have a measurable advantage over the market, competitors, or environment.
2. Quantify probabilities and expected payoffs wherever possible.
3. Allocate resources proportionally to the size of the edge, avoiding overexposure to uncertain or negative expectancy outcomes.

This mindset encourages discipline: you act only when a favorable risk-reward relationship exists, rather than chasing action for the sake of activity.

Applications in Probabilistic Decision-Making

- **Investing:** Allocate capital to investments where your research or insights provide an informational or probabilistic advantage. Use Kelly-like sizing to manage exposure.
- **Entrepreneurship:** Commit resources to projects with the highest expected return relative to risk, while maintaining flexibility to pivot.
- **Sports, Poker, and Games:** Bet or act proportionally to the calculated advantage, optimizing long-term growth while minimizing the risk of ruin.
- **Personal Decisions:** Evaluate opportunities (career moves, education, ventures) in terms of expected value and allocate time, effort, and resources accordingly.

Psychological and Strategic Benefits

- **Reduces overexposure:** Prevents catastrophic losses by calibrating bet size to probability and payoff.
- **Enhances compounding:** Optimizes long-term growth by allocating more to high-edge opportunities.
- **Encourages disciplined thinking:** Focuses attention on favorable probabilistic situations rather than impulsive actions.
- **Bridges theory and practice:** Combines mathematical rigor with real-world application, creating a systematic approach to uncertainty.

Key Takeaways

- The Kelly Criterion provides a mathematical framework for optimal bet sizing based on probability and payoff.
- Edge-based frameworks emphasize acting only where you have a measurable advantage.
- Together, they guide resource allocation, risk management, and long-term compounding in uncertain environments.
- Mastery of these frameworks cultivates discipline, strategic clarity, and a probabilistic edge across investing, entrepreneurship, and personal decision-making.

By integrating Kelly sizing with edge-based thinking, you gain the ability to act decisively in uncertain environments, maximizing expected outcomes while controlling downside risk. In probabilistic decision-making, knowing both *what* to bet on and *how much* is the difference between fleeting success and sustained, compounding advantage.

Chapter 10

Emotional Discipline Detachment

In a world governed by uncertainty, outcomes are never guaranteed. Even the most meticulously calculated decisions can yield unexpected results. Emotional discipline and detachment are the mental frameworks that allow us to navigate this uncertainty without being overwhelmed by fear, greed, or frustration.

This chapter explores how to separate outcomes from process, build resilience against randomness, and use detachment as a competitive advantage. By mastering these skills, you not only protect yourself from emotional pitfalls but also make clearer, more rational, and probabilistically sound decisions in life, investing, and business.

10.1 Separating Outcomes from Process

One of the most powerful yet often overlooked mental skills in probabilistic decision-making is the ability to distinguish between the quality of your decisions and the results they produce. Too often, we equate a favorable outcome with a good decision and a negative outcome with a bad decision. This conflation is a trap, especially in high-uncertainty environments where luck, randomness, and variance can dominate results.

The Core Idea

Separating outcomes from process means evaluating the *decision-making process itself* rather than judging solely by the outcome. A decision can be rational, well-informed, and based on positive expected value, yet still fail due to randomness. Conversely, a poor decision might succeed temporarily because of luck. The key is to focus on whether your approach consistently maximizes expected value, manages risk, and adheres to probabilistic reasoning.

Why This Separation Matters

- **Reduces emotional volatility:** You remain calm and objective when results fluctuate, preventing impulsive reactions like chasing losses or abandoning sound strategies.
- **Encourages long-term thinking:** Focusing on process over outcomes promotes compounding mental and financial edge.
- **Improves learning:** By analyzing decisions independently of outcomes, you can identify what worked, what didn't, and why accelerating skill development.
- **Mitigates bias:** Outcome bias, luck attribution, and hindsight bias are minimized, allowing more accurate assessment of decision quality.

Practical Applications

- **Investing:** A trader may lose money on a trade despite thorough research, sound risk management, and proper position sizing. Evaluating the decision process helps identify what was done correctly and ensures consistency in future trades.
- **Entrepreneurship:** A startup may fail due to market timing or macroeconomic conditions beyond the founder's control. Reviewing the quality of strategic decisions, team execution, and customer feedback is more instructive than fixating on failure.
- **Personal Life:** Career moves, relationship choices, or health decisions often produce unpredictable outcomes. Evaluating whether you made well-reasoned, values-aligned choices reinforces discipline and confidence regardless of results.

Steps to Apply Outcome-Process Separation

1. **Define a decision framework:** Identify clear criteria, rules, and expected value principles to guide your choices.
2. **Document your reasoning:** Record assumptions, analysis, and alternatives considered before acting.

3. **Evaluate process independently:** After outcomes unfold, review whether decisions adhered to your framework, irrespective of results.

4. **Learn and iterate:** Adjust the process only when errors in reasoning, assumptions, or information quality are identified not merely because of unfavorable outcomes.

5. **Normalize variance:** Accept that randomness and variance are inherent; focus on process integrity over outcome fluctuations.

Psychological and Strategic Benefits

- **Emotional resilience:** Shields you from anxiety, regret, and impulsive reactions caused by unpredictable results.
- **Consistency:** Reinforces disciplined decision-making habits that compound over time.
- **Enhanced probabilistic reasoning:** Encourages focusing on expected value, variance, and risk management.
- **Sustainable success:** Reduces the likelihood of abandoning sound strategies due to short-term unfavorable outcomes.

Key Takeaways

- Good decisions can fail; bad decisions can succeed. Judging solely by outcomes is misleading.
- Evaluate decisions based on process quality, adherence to probabilistic reasoning, and risk management.
- Separating outcomes from process cultivates emotional discipline, learning, and long-term resilience.
- This mindset transforms randomness from a source of stress into an opportunity for strategic advantage.

By mastering the separation of outcomes from process, you gain the clarity to act decisively in uncertainty, remain calm amid fluctuations, and continuously refine your decision-making skills ultimately turning probabilistic thinking into a sustainable competitive edge.

10.2 Resilience Against Randomness

In probabilistic environments, randomness is inevitable. Even the most carefully calculated decisions can produce unexpected outcomes due to chance, variance, or events beyond one's control. Resilience against randomness is the mental and strategic capacity to endure, adapt, and even thrive in the face of unpredictable outcomes. It is the hallmark of probabilistic thinkers who succeed over the long term, not by avoiding uncertainty, but by preparing for it mentally and operationally.

The Core Idea

Resilience against randomness involves three interrelated components:

1. **Acceptance:** Understanding that uncertainty, luck, and variance are intrinsic to complex systems.
2. **Adaptation:** Developing flexible strategies and processes that can absorb shocks without collapsing.
3. **Persistence:** Continuing to act according to sound probabilistic principles despite temporary setbacks or unfavorable outcomes.

Rather than attempting to control randomness which is impossible resilient individuals focus on what is controllable: their decision-making process, risk management, and capacity to respond effectively to unexpected events.

Why Resilience Matters

- **Mitigates emotional volatility:** Reduces panic, frustration, and impulsive reactions when outcomes deviate from expectations.
- **Preserves long-term capital:** In investing or entrepreneurship, avoiding ruin and maintaining operational flexibility is critical to survival.
- **Supports continuous learning:** Setbacks become valuable feedback rather than demoralizing failures.
- **Enhances probabilistic reasoning:** A resilient mindset allows clearer analysis by separating luck from skill, avoiding bias in evaluating outcomes.

Practical Strategies for Building Resilience

- **Diversification:** Spread risk across multiple independent bets, investments, or projects to reduce vulnerability to any single adverse event.
- **Position sizing and limits:** Avoid overexposure; commit only a calculated portion of resources to each probabilistic opportunity.
- **Stress-testing decisions:** Evaluate how strategies perform under extreme scenarios, including tail events and unexpected shocks.
- **Process over outcome focus:** Maintain discipline in decision-making even when randomness produces temporary losses.
- **Mental rehearsal and scenario planning:** Anticipate potential surprises and visualize appropriate responses to reduce emotional impact when they occur.

Applications Across Domains

- **Investing:** Portfolio managers use hedging, diversification, and risk budgeting to withstand market volatility while maintaining exposure to positive expected value opportunities.
- **Entrepreneurship:** Startups embrace optionality, test minimum viable products, and iterate based on feedback to remain resilient amid unpredictable market conditions.
- **Personal Life:** Individuals maintain emotional equilibrium and flexibility in career, relationships, and health decisions despite setbacks or uncertainty.

Psychological and Strategic Benefits

- **Reduces stress and anxiety:** Acceptance of randomness decreases emotional reactivity.
- **Encourages long-term focus:** Resilience allows sustained action toward goals despite short-term fluctuations.
- **Improves adaptability:** Flexible strategies enable quick adjustment when the environment changes.
- **Strengthens probabilistic judgment:** Consistently acting in line with expected value enhances long-term outcomes.

Key Takeaways

- Randomness is unavoidable; resisting or ignoring it leads to poor decision-making and emotional strain.
- Resilience is built through acceptance, adaptation, and disciplined persistence.
- Diversification, risk management, stress-testing, and process-focused thinking are essential strategies.
- Cultivating resilience transforms randomness from a threat into a source of opportunity and competitive advantage.

Ultimately, resilience against randomness is not about predicting every possible outcome it is about preparing to endure and capitalize on uncertainty. By embracing this mindset, you gain the mental and strategic flexibility to navigate complexity, protect yourself from catastrophic losses, and thrive in a probabilistic world.

10.3 Detachment as a Competitive Edge

Detachment is the deliberate practice of maintaining emotional equilibrium and objective judgment, even when outcomes, stakes, or external pressures are high. In probabilistic decision-making, detachment is not indifference; it is the ability to act with clarity, discipline, and rationality without being swayed by fear, greed, or the immediate emotional impact of results. By cultivating detachment, you transform uncertainty and volatility into strategic advantages.

The Core Idea

Detachment allows you to separate yourself psychologically from short-term outcomes while remaining fully engaged in the decision-making process. This separation creates a mental buffer that prevents impulsive reactions and encourages consistent application of probabilistic principles. Detached thinkers focus on:

- Process over outcome
- Expected value over luck-driven results
- Long-term compounding over short-term wins or losses

This mindset enables superior decision-making in environments where variance, randomness, and uncertainty dominate.

Why Detachment Matters

- **Reduces emotional biases:** Detachment minimizes the influence of overconfidence, loss aversion, and outcome bias.
- **Enhances clarity:** By observing situations objectively, you better identify patterns, edges, and opportunities.
- **Improves consistency:** Actions are guided by rational analysis and probabilistic thinking rather than reactive emotions.
- **Strengthens resilience:** Detachment allows you to withstand losses or setbacks without panic, preserving the ability to act effectively.

Practical Applications

- **Investing:** Detached investors stick to their strategy during market volatility, avoiding panic selling or impulsive buying based on emotions.
- **Entrepreneurship:** Founders remain committed to validated strategies while remaining flexible to pivot when data indicates necessary changes, rather than reacting emotionally to temporary setbacks.
- **Negotiation:** Detachment allows you to negotiate without attachment to ego or immediate outcomes, leading to better long-term agreements.
- **Personal Life:** Detachment in decision-making helps maintain composure in relationships, career transitions, and life planning, allowing objective evaluation of risks and rewards.

Steps to Cultivate Detachment

1. **Recognize emotional triggers:** Identify situations where you are prone to react impulsively or irrationally.
2. **Focus on process:** Evaluate decisions based on preparation, reasoning, and probabilistic assessment rather than immediate results.
3. **Practice mindfulness and reflection:** Regularly observe your thoughts and emotions without judgment to build self-awareness.
4. **Set rules and frameworks:** Establish pre-defined guidelines and decision protocols that you follow regardless of short-term outcomes.
5. **Learn from randomness:** Treat unexpected outcomes as feedback, not personal failure, reinforcing disciplined adaptation.

Psychological and Strategic Benefits

- **Reduces stress and anxiety:** Emotional separation from results prevents reactive panic and fear-driven decisions.
- **Enhances rational judgment:** Clear-minded decision-making improves the quality and consistency of actions.
- **Strengthens competitive advantage:** While others are emotionally reactive, detached thinkers act with foresight, composure, and strategic discipline.
- **Supports long-term compounding:** Staying disciplined through variance ensures repeated positive expected value actions accumulate over time.

Key Takeaways

- Detachment is a conscious mental skill, not emotional indifference.
- It allows you to act rationally and probabilistically in the face of uncertainty.
- Applying detachment reduces emotional biases, improves decision consistency, and enhances resilience.
- When combined with emotional discipline, detachment transforms randomness and volatility into a strategic competitive edge.

By mastering detachment, you gain the mental clarity and strategic composure to make superior decisions in uncertain environments. This ability to remain calm, objective, and process-focused under pressure is a rare yet powerful advantage that differentiates probabilistic thinkers from those swayed by emotions and short-term outcomes.

Part III

Applications of the Probabilistic Mindset

Chapter 11

Personal Life Choices

Every day, we make decisions that shape the trajectory of our lives what career to pursue, who to spend time with, how to care for our health. Each choice carries uncertainty, and yet, most people treat these decisions as deterministic, expecting predictable outcomes.

This chapter explores how to apply a probabilistic mindset to personal life choices. We will examine how careers can be approached as bets with varying risks and rewards, how relationships and social networks compound over time, and how health decisions can be optimized by balancing risk and habit. By viewing life through the lens of probability, you gain the ability to make smarter, more resilient choices that maximize long-term value and personal growth.

11.1 Career as a Probabilistic Bet

Choosing a career is one of the most consequential decisions in life, yet it is often approached with deterministic thinking: "If I study X, I will become Y." In reality, career outcomes are uncertain, influenced by market shifts, technological changes, competition, timing, and even luck. Viewing your career as a probabilistic bet allows you to make decisions that optimize long-term expected value rather than chase certainty.

The Core Idea

A probabilistic career mindset treats each choice job offers, projects, skill investments, networking as a bet with potential payoffs and risks. Instead of expecting guaranteed outcomes, you focus on:

- **Expected value:** Which career paths or opportunities maximize your long-term upside?

- **Optionality:** Which decisions keep multiple future paths open, allowing you to pivot if conditions change?
- **Edge:** Where do you have unique skills, knowledge, or insights that increase the likelihood of success?
- **Risk management:** How can you structure your choices to avoid catastrophic failure while pursuing high-reward opportunities?

By thinking probabilistically, you stop treating failure as a personal flaw and start seeing it as a natural outcome in high-variance systems. You learn to hedge bets, experiment, and iterate toward long-term growth.

Applying Probabilistic Thinking to Career Choices

- **Skill investments:** Focus on rare and transferable skills that provide a competitive edge and optionality across industries.
- **Multiple pathways:** Diversify your experience through side projects, freelance work, or parallel learning to increase flexibility.
- **Networking as leverage:** Build relationships strategically; a strong network increases access to high-value opportunities, often in unpredictable ways.
- **Experimentation:** Treat new roles, industries, or ventures as small-scale bets to gather information and test fit before committing fully.
- **Timing and momentum:** Recognize that early bets may pay off later; consistently making high-probability decisions compounds over time.

Psychological and Strategic Benefits

- **Reduces fear of failure:** Understanding that variance is natural in careers allows you to take calculated risks.
- **Encourages long-term thinking:** You focus on compounding skills, knowledge, and networks over decades rather than immediate outcomes.
- **Improves adaptability:** Probabilistic thinking prepares you to pivot when circumstances or industries shift.
- **Enhances decision quality:** Each career move is assessed based on expected value, optionality, and edge, not just short-term rewards.

Key Takeaways

- Careers are complex, uncertain systems; deterministic planning often leads to disappointment.
- Treat each choice as a probabilistic bet, balancing risk, expected value, and optionality.
- Invest in rare skills, experiment with opportunities, and build networks to increase your long-term upside.
- Embrace failure and variance as natural outcomes, focusing on process and decision quality rather than immediate results.

By framing your career as a series of probabilistic bets, you transform uncertainty from a source of anxiety into a strategic advantage. Over time, this mindset allows you to accumulate skills, experiences, and relationships that compound, maximizing your chances of achieving meaningful, high-impact outcomes.

11.2 Relationships & Social Networks as Compounding Systems

Human connections are among the most powerful compounding forces in life. Just as money compounds through investment over time, relationships personal, professional, and social can create exponential value when nurtured strategically and authentically. By viewing relationships as probabilistic and compounding systems, you can prioritize meaningful interactions, build trust, and generate opportunities that multiply over the long term.

The Core Idea

A relationship or social connection is not a static asset; it evolves over time and interacts with other relationships in a network. Compounding occurs when positive interactions, trust, and reciprocity accumulate, creating leverage that extends beyond individual connections. This approach requires seeing social networks not merely as a collection of contacts, but as systems where:

- **Actions multiply:** Helping, mentoring, or collaborating with others increases the likelihood of receiving support, referrals, and opportunities in return.
- **Trust compounds:** Consistency, integrity, and reliability amplify influence and credibility across the network.

- **Diverse connections increase optionality:** A broad yet meaningful network exposes you to new ideas, perspectives, and possibilities you cannot foresee individually.

In essence, relationships are probabilistic bets: the more positive interactions and high-quality connections you cultivate, the greater the expected long-term payoff.

Applying Probabilistic Thinking to Relationships

- **Invest early and consistently:** Nurture friendships, mentors, and professional connections proactively, even when immediate benefits are not apparent.
- **Prioritize high-value connections:** Focus on individuals and communities where mutual growth, shared values, and complementary skills create the greatest expected value.
- **Reciprocate and add value:** Contributions whether guidance, resources, or support compound trust and strengthen long-term bonds.
- **Diversify social exposure:** Engage with a variety of networks, industries, and cultures to increase optionality and reduce dependence on any single social channel.
- **Monitor network health:** Identify relationships that are negative, toxic, or draining, and reallocate your time and energy toward those with higher long-term payoff.

Social Networks as Probabilistic Systems

Social networks behave like complex adaptive systems: each node (individual) interacts with others in dynamic, often unpredictable ways. Small actions introductions, thoughtful advice, or consistent support can trigger cascading effects, resulting in opportunities or insights far beyond what a single interaction might suggest. By understanding these dynamics:

- You recognize that not all relationships produce immediate results.
- You cultivate patience, focusing on long-term growth rather than short-term returns.
- You position yourself to capitalize on serendipity and emergent opportunities that arise unpredictably within the network.

Psychological and Strategic Benefits

- **Leverage and influence:** Strong networks amplify your ability to access knowledge, capital, and opportunities.
- **Resilience:** Diverse and supportive relationships help buffer against personal, professional, or economic setbacks.
- **Exponential growth potential:** Positive compounding in networks creates returns that grow faster than linear effort alone.
- **Enhanced learning and perspective:** Engaging with diverse individuals increases insight, creativity, and probabilistic reasoning.

Key Takeaways

- Treat relationships as probabilistic, compounding systems rather than isolated interactions.
- Consistent investment in trust, reciprocity, and high-value connections yields exponential long-term benefits.
- Diversifying social networks increases optionality and exposure to unexpected opportunities.
- Recognize that small, thoughtful actions can trigger cascading effects that multiply influence, learning, and opportunity.

By embracing a probabilistic and compounding perspective on relationships, you transform networking from a transactional activity into a long-term strategy. Over time, your social capital grows exponentially, amplifying opportunities, resilience, and impact across both personal and professional spheres.

11.3 Health: Balancing Risks and Habits

Health is often the most undervalued yet essential asset in life. Like wealth or relationships, it is subject to uncertainty, randomness, and long-term compounding effects. Small daily choices diet, exercise, sleep, stress management interact with unpredictable external factors such as genetics, accidents, or environmental risks. Adopting a probabilistic mindset toward health allows you to make decisions that maximize long-term well-being, minimize catastrophic risks, and build sustainable habits that compound over time.

The Core Idea

Balancing health is not about perfect control or eliminating all risks; it is about making informed choices that increase expected outcomes while managing downside exposure. Health decisions can be approached probabilistically in three dimensions:

- **Preventive measures:** Actions that reduce the probability of adverse events, such as vaccinations, regular check-ups, and balanced nutrition.
- **Risk management:** Identifying high-variance activities (extreme sports, fad diets, overwork) and controlling exposure to avoid catastrophic outcomes.
- **Habit compounding:** Small, consistent routines exercise, sleep hygiene, mindfulness that produce long-term benefits far beyond immediate effects.

By evaluating health decisions through expected value and variance, you can prioritize actions that yield maximum benefit while limiting irreversible consequences.

Applying Probabilistic Thinking to Health

- **Exercise:** Focus on consistent moderate activity that provides high expected value strengthening cardiovascular and musculoskeletal systems rather than chasing extreme performance for short-term reward.
- **Nutrition:** Adopt a diet that balances macronutrients, micronutrients, and moderation. Avoid extreme fad diets with unpredictable outcomes.
- **Sleep:** Prioritize regular sleep schedules to maximize cognitive function, immune health, and emotional resilience, recognizing that even small deviations can compound over time.
- **Mental health:** Engage in practices like mindfulness, meditation, and stress management to reduce long-term risk of burnout, anxiety, or depression.
- **Medical check-ups and preventive care:** Use screening and diagnostics to detect early warning signs, reducing the probability of catastrophic health events.

Health as a Probabilistic System

Your body and mind are complex adaptive systems. Outcomes longevity, vitality, or cognitive performance result from the interaction of countless variables, including lifestyle choices, genetics, environment, and randomness. Probabilistic thinking encourages:

- **Focus on process over isolated outcomes:** One unhealthy meal or skipped workout does not define your health trajectory; cumulative patterns do.
- **Risk-awareness:** Understand which behaviors carry high variance or catastrophic potential and mitigate them.
- **Incremental improvements:** Small, consistent positive habits compound exponentially, producing outsized long-term benefits.

Psychological and Strategic Benefits

- **Reduces health anxiety:** Probabilistic thinking reframes occasional setbacks as natural variance rather than failure.
- **Promotes consistency:** Emphasizing daily habits over perfection leads to sustainable improvements.
- **Enhances decision quality:** Understanding trade-offs between risk and reward allows smarter lifestyle choices.
- **Maximizes longevity and vitality:** Incremental, evidence-based decisions produce long-term compounding effects on health outcomes.

Key Takeaways

- Health decisions are probabilistic; small, consistent actions compound over time.
- Focus on preventive measures, risk management, and habit formation rather than attempting perfect control.
- Understand the variance and uncertainty inherent in health outcomes, and design routines that maximize expected value while minimizing catastrophic risks.
- By balancing risk and habits intelligently, you create a foundation for long-term vitality, resilience, and the capacity to pursue other high-value life goals.

Approaching health as a probabilistic system empowers you to make rational, high-expected-value decisions that compound over time. Just as with career and relationships, consistency, risk-awareness, and process-focused thinking transform uncertainty from a source of anxiety into a strategic advantage for long-term well-being.

Chapter 12

Investing Finance

Investing is the quintessential probabilistic game. Every decision whether allocating capital to stocks, bonds, startups, or alternative assets carries uncertainty. Unlike deterministic thinking, which assumes predictable outcomes, a probabilistic approach acknowledges the inherent randomness of markets, the asymmetry of risk and reward, and the compounding nature of repeated decisions.

This chapter explores how to design portfolios with probabilistic thinking, structure asymmetric risk-reward setups, and navigate market volatility. By embracing uncertainty rather than fearing it, investors can improve decision quality, preserve capital, and maximize long-term expected returns. The principles here apply not only to finance but to any situation where risk, reward, and uncertainty intersect.

12.1 Probabilistic Portfolio Design

Traditional portfolio design often relies on deterministic assumptions: expected returns, historical averages, or simplistic risk metrics. While these methods provide a baseline, they fail to fully account for the randomness, variance, and tail risks inherent in financial markets. A probabilistic portfolio design, in contrast, treats each asset and allocation as a set of possible outcomes, weighted by probability, and focuses on maximizing expected value while controlling downside exposure.

The Core Idea

A probabilistic portfolio is constructed around three guiding principles:

1. **Diversification across independent bets:** Spread capital across assets whose outcomes are not perfectly correlated, reducing the probability of simultaneous losses.

2. **Asymmetric risk-reward allocation:** Favor investments where the potential upside significantly outweighs the downside, even if the probability of success is moderate.

3. **Continuous adjustment and learning:** Update allocations as new information emerges, using probabilistic reasoning rather than reacting emotionally to short-term market movements.

By designing a portfolio with these principles, investors move from a focus on predicting exact outcomes to managing exposure to variance and maximizing long-term compounding.

Steps to Build a Probabilistic Portfolio

1. **Identify potential bets:** Assess a wide range of assets, sectors, or strategies based on expected value, variance, and correlation.

2. **Estimate probabilities and payoffs:** Consider historical data, fundamental analysis, and scenario planning to approximate likelihoods and magnitudes of outcomes.

3. **Construct the allocation:** Combine assets in a way that balances risk, preserves optionality, and emphasizes asymmetric opportunities.

4. **Stress-test the portfolio:** Simulate extreme scenarios and tail events to understand vulnerabilities and make necessary adjustments.

5. **Monitor and update:** Reassess probabilities, correlations, and expected values periodically, adjusting allocations as the environment evolves.

Principles in Practice

- **Diversification:** Don't rely on a single stock, sector, or asset class; ensure that losses in one area are unlikely to wipe out gains elsewhere.

- **Optionality:** Include assets or strategies with unlimited or high upside relative to their cost or downside risk.

- **Position sizing:** Allocate capital proportional to edge and variance; smaller allocations for high-risk bets, larger for high-confidence opportunities.

- **Rebalancing:** Adjust positions to maintain probabilistic balance rather than chasing short-term gains or reacting to volatility.

Psychological and Strategic Benefits

- **Reduces emotional bias:** Probabilistic thinking shifts focus from daily market noise to long-term expected outcomes.
- **Preserves capital:** Diversification and tail-risk management protect against catastrophic losses.
- **Enhances compounding:** Consistent application of high expected value decisions allows wealth to grow exponentially over time.
- **Improves adaptability:** Regular updates and scenario analysis prepare the portfolio for changing market conditions.

Key Takeaways

- A probabilistic portfolio treats uncertainty as an opportunity, not a threat.
- Focus on diversification, asymmetry, and expected value rather than deterministic predictions.
- Small, disciplined allocations to high-edge opportunities, combined with protective measures against downside risk, create long-term compounding advantages.
- Continuous monitoring, learning, and adjustment ensure the portfolio remains robust under changing conditions.

By designing portfolios probabilistically, you shift the mindset from "trying to predict the market" to "managing exposure intelligently." Over time, this approach not only preserves capital but positions you to capitalize on the unpredictable nature of financial markets, turning randomness into a strategic advantage.

12.2 Asymmetric Risk-Reward Setups

In investing and finance, not all opportunities are created equal. Some bets offer limited upside but high downside, while others provide small probability of success with enormous potential payoff. Understanding and structuring asymmetric risk-reward setups is essential for maximizing long-term expected value and compounding returns under uncertainty.

The Core Idea

An asymmetric risk-reward setup occurs when the potential upside of an investment significantly outweighs its potential downside. Probabilistic thinking focuses on identifying these opportunities and allocating capital in a way that:

- Protects against large losses (limited downside)
- Exposes you to outsized gains (high upside)
- Favors repeated small bets that collectively compound over time

By systematically seeking asymmetry, investors shift the odds in their favor, even when outcomes are uncertain or variable.

Examples of Asymmetric Setups

- **Startups and venture investing:** A small investment in a high-potential startup may have limited downside (the capital invested) but enormous upside if the company succeeds.
- **Options and derivatives:** Using limited capital to gain exposure to large price movements allows risk-limited positions with potentially exponential returns.
- **Skill-based advantages:** Investing time or resources where you have a unique edge creates asymmetric payoffs relative to competitors without that edge.
- **Optionality in business decisions:** Structuring agreements, partnerships, or projects with upside flexibility but controlled downside.

Designing Asymmetric Bets

1. **Identify high-upside opportunities:** Seek investments, projects, or decisions with potential payoffs that are multiple times your initial exposure.
2. **Quantify downside risk:** Determine the maximum potential loss and ensure it is acceptable relative to your capital and risk tolerance.
3. **Size positions appropriately:** Allocate capital proportionally to expected value, edge, and probability of success.
4. **Diversify across asymmetric bets:** Avoid overconcentration; spread small positions across multiple high-expected-value opportunities.

5. **Iterate and adapt:** Monitor outcomes, learn from results, and continuously refine your ability to identify asymmetric opportunities.

Psychological and Strategic Benefits

- **Maximizes expected value:** Even if most bets fail, the rare wins can dominate long-term performance.
- **Reduces fear of loss:** Knowing that downside is limited allows you to take high-upside opportunities with confidence.
- **Encourages disciplined risk-taking:** Focus shifts from avoiding all risk to selectively engaging in favorable asymmetry.
- **Supports compounding:** Repeated small asymmetric bets accumulate into significant long-term gains.

Key Takeaways

- Seek opportunities where potential rewards substantially exceed potential losses.
- Carefully quantify downside, size positions intelligently, and diversify across multiple asymmetric bets.
- Treat asymmetric setups as probabilistic engines for long-term compounding.
- Over time, disciplined asymmetric investing allows you to thrive in uncertainty, turning randomness into advantage.

By consistently identifying and exploiting asymmetric risk-reward setups, investors create a systematic framework for compounding returns. Rather than attempting to predict every market movement, this approach focuses on positioning capital where upside dominates downside, allowing uncertainty itself to become a source of opportunity.

12.3 Surviving Downturns and Volatility

Financial markets are inherently volatile. Prices fluctuate, economies cycle, and unexpected events from geopolitical crises to technological disruptions can trigger sharp downturns. Even the most carefully constructed portfolios can experience losses. A probabilistic mindset equips investors not only to survive these fluctuations but to thrive over the long term by understanding risk, preparing for uncertainty, and maintaining discipline.

The Core Idea

Volatility is the manifestation of uncertainty in markets. While short-term movements may seem chaotic, the long-term outcome depends on how you structure exposure, manage risk, and respond to unexpected events. Survival during downturns is as important, if not more so, than chasing high returns because catastrophic losses are difficult, if not impossible, to recover from.

Key principles include:

- **Risk management over prediction:** You cannot predict every market shock, but you can limit exposure to irreversible losses.
- **Capital preservation:** Protecting principal ensures that you can continue to participate in future opportunities.
- **Emotional discipline:** Maintaining composure prevents impulsive decisions that exacerbate losses.

Practical Strategies to Survive Volatility

1. **Diversification:** Spread investments across uncorrelated asset classes, sectors, and geographies to reduce the likelihood of simultaneous losses.
2. **Cash reserves and liquidity:** Maintain sufficient liquidity to weather downturns, enabling you to capitalize on opportunities when others are forced to sell.
3. **Position sizing:** Avoid overconcentration in any single investment; limit exposure according to risk tolerance and variance.
4. **Hedging:** Use financial instruments or alternative strategies to mitigate downside in volatile conditions.
5. **Focus on high-edge investments:** During volatility, the relative advantage of well-researched, high-expectancy positions becomes more pronounced.
6. **Long-term perspective:** Recognize that temporary declines are often noise; focus on process and expected value over short-term results.

Psychological Resilience in Volatile Markets

Volatility tests both portfolios and the investor's mindset. Emotional reactions panic selling, overleveraging, or chasing trends can convert temporary losses into permanent setbacks. A probabilistic approach fosters:

- **Acceptance of uncertainty:** Understanding that short-term swings are natural reduces stress and overreaction.
- **Discipline:** Probabilistic frameworks provide objective criteria for making decisions, minimizing emotional interference.
- **Patience:** Maintaining a long-term horizon allows compounding to work despite interim volatility.
- **Learning orientation:** Treating downturns as opportunities for observation and data collection improves future decision-making.

Key Takeaways

- Volatility is inevitable; survival depends on preparation, risk management, and emotional discipline.
- Diversification, liquidity, hedging, and position sizing reduce downside exposure.
- Long-term perspective and patience allow probabilistic advantages to compound despite short-term fluctuations.
- Downturns can become opportunities if approached strategically rather than emotionally.

By embracing probabilistic thinking in the face of market volatility, investors shift focus from attempting to predict every outcome to managing exposure intelligently. This mindset turns uncertainty into an ally, preserving capital, enabling long-term compounding, and positioning you to capitalize on opportunities that others miss in panic or shortsightedness.

Chapter 13

Entrepreneurship Innovation

Entrepreneurship is the ultimate high-variance endeavor. Unlike conventional employment, where outcomes are relatively predictable, startups and innovation ventures operate in a world of uncertainty, asymmetric payoffs, and complex interdependencies. Success is rarely linear; a single breakthrough can generate outsized returns, while countless small failures quietly fade away.

This chapter explores how probabilistic thinking can guide entrepreneurs to structure ventures intelligently, manage risk, and capture optionality. By embracing uncertainty, designing minimum viable bets, and building diversified innovation portfolios, founders and innovators can maximize the probability of meaningful success while surviving inevitable setbacks.

13.1 Startups as High-Variance Systems

Startups are inherently high-variance systems, meaning that their outcomes are widely distributed and often unpredictable. Unlike established businesses, where revenue streams and operational patterns are relatively stable, startups operate in environments with extreme uncertainty, rapidly changing variables, and non-linear feedback loops. This high variance is what makes entrepreneurship both risky and potentially transformative: a single successful startup can generate outsized returns that dwarf the combined outcomes of many smaller, safer ventures.

The Nature of Variance in Startups

High-variance systems exhibit the following characteristics:

- **Non-linear outcomes:** Small differences in execution, timing, or market conditions can lead to exponentially different results. A minor pivot or feature change can turn failure into runaway success or vice versa.

- **Extreme asymmetry:** Most startups fail or produce modest returns, but a small minority achieve massive scale, creating asymmetric payoff distributions.
- **Interconnected risks:** Factors such as team dynamics, market trends, investor sentiment, and regulatory changes interact in unpredictable ways, amplifying uncertainty.
- **Feedback loops:** Success breeds visibility, resources, and talent, which further accelerate growth, while failure can compound challenges and reduce optionality.

Understanding startups as high-variance systems shifts the focus from attempting precise predictions to managing exposure, maximizing optionality, and embracing probabilistic thinking.

Applying Probabilistic Thinking to Startups

- **Embrace uncertainty:** Accept that precise outcomes are unknowable and that failure is a natural part of the system.
- **Focus on expected value, not certainty:** Prioritize ideas, strategies, and experiments where potential upside significantly outweighs downside, even if success is uncertain.
- **Iterative experimentation:** Use rapid cycles of testing, learning, and adaptation to gather information and adjust strategies based on probabilistic outcomes.
- **Portfolio mindset:** Treat a series of bets or experiments as a collective system; the success of one high-upside experiment can more than compensate for multiple smaller failures.
- **Optionality preservation:** Structure decisions to maintain flexibility, allowing pivots, strategic partnerships, or scaling opportunities when favorable conditions emerge.

Psychological and Strategic Benefits

- **Resilience against failure:** Understanding that volatility is natural reduces fear and emotional overreaction.
- **Enhanced decision-making:** Probabilistic reasoning encourages rational allocation of capital, time, and resources, focusing on high-expected-value initiatives.

- **Leverage asymmetry:** By seeking opportunities with large upside relative to limited downside, entrepreneurs can maximize long-term compounding potential.
- **Adaptive growth:** Viewing startups as dynamic, high-variance systems fosters agility, innovation, and the ability to capitalize on emergent opportunities.

Key Takeaways

- Startups are high-variance systems with non-linear outcomes, extreme asymmetry, and unpredictable dynamics.
- Probabilistic thinking allows entrepreneurs to embrace uncertainty, focus on expected value, and design experiments that maximize upside.
- A portfolio approach diversifying bets, preserving optionality, and iterating rapidly enhances the likelihood of outsized success.
- Psychological resilience, disciplined decision-making, and strategic flexibility are crucial for thriving in high-variance entrepreneurial environments.

By framing startups as high-variance systems, founders shift from fearing uncertainty to leveraging it. Every decision becomes a probabilistic bet, where intelligent risk-taking, learning, and optionality compound over time, transforming volatility from a threat into a source of opportunity and growth.

13.2 Minimum Viable Bets (MVBs)

In the high-variance world of startups, every decision is a bet. Yet, not all bets need to be all-in. The concept of **Minimum Viable Bets (MVBs)** is a cornerstone of probabilistic entrepreneurship. An MVB is a small, controlled experiment designed to test a hypothesis or explore an opportunity while minimizing downside and preserving optionality. Unlike large-scale, high-risk commitments, MVBs allow entrepreneurs to learn, iterate, and adapt without jeopardizing the entire venture.

The Core Philosophy

MVBs embody three fundamental principles:

1. **Controlled exposure:** Allocate only a fraction of resources capital, time, or effort so that failure does not threaten the overall system.

2. **Maximized learning:** Even if the bet fails, it yields critical insights that guide future decisions.
3. **Optionality creation:** Success provides scalable opportunities, while failure preserves the flexibility to pivot, exit, or explore alternative pathways.

By structuring ventures as a series of MVBs, entrepreneurs transform uncertainty into manageable experiments, systematically increasing the probability of long-term success.

Why MVBs Are Essential

Startups are complex systems with high variance, meaning outcomes are unpredictable and often non-linear. MVBs help founders navigate this uncertainty by:

- **Testing assumptions efficiently:** Validate hypotheses about customers, markets, or technology without committing excessive resources.
- **Limiting catastrophic failure:** By keeping bets small, entrepreneurs reduce the risk of irrecoverable losses.
- **Accelerating learning cycles:** Rapid experimentation provides actionable data to refine strategy and decision-making.
- **Preserving strategic flexibility:** Optionality allows for pivots, scaling successful experiments, or reallocating resources based on evidence.

Designing Effective MVBs

To implement MVBs successfully, consider the following framework:

1. **Define the hypothesis:** Clearly articulate the assumption being tested, e.g., "Customers will pay $X for feature Y."
2. **Set measurable success criteria:** Identify specific outcomes that indicate whether the hypothesis is valid.
3. **Commit minimal resources:** Limit capital, time, and effort to the smallest amount necessary to gain meaningful insights.
4. **Execute rapidly:** The value of an MVB lies in fast feedback and early learning avoid prolonged, resource-heavy development.
5. **Analyze and iterate:** Use the results to update beliefs and inform the next bet, applying probabilistic reasoning and Bayesian updates when possible.

Real-World Examples

- **Product testing:** Launching a prototype, landing page, or limited batch to measure customer interest before full-scale production.
- **Market experiments:** Offering a service to a select demographic or region to gauge adoption rates.
- **Team structure experiments:** Trialing a new workflow or small cross-functional team before wider implementation.
- **Seed investments:** Small, diversified investments in multiple ventures instead of a single large commitment.

Psychological and Strategic Advantages

- **Reduces fear of failure:** Smaller bets are less threatening, encouraging experimentation.
- **Promotes disciplined risk-taking:** Focus shifts from reckless risk to high-expected-value decisions.
- **Accelerates learning and adaptation:** Early feedback refines strategies and informs future bets.
- **Maintains flexibility:** Optionality ensures the ability to pivot or scale, turning uncertainty into a strategic advantage.

Key Takeaways

- Minimum Viable Bets allow entrepreneurs to experiment with limited downside and high learning potential.
- They transform uncertainty into a systematic, iterative process that increases the likelihood of long-term success.
- MVBs preserve optionality, allowing ventures to pivot, scale, or reallocate resources based on evidence.
- Over time, a series of intelligently structured MVBs compounds knowledge, opportunity, and strategic advantage, creating a resilient foundation for entrepreneurial success.

By adopting MVBs, founders shift from fear-driven decision-making to a disciplined, probabilistic approach. Each small, calculated experiment becomes a stepping stone, providing insights, flexibility, and optionality while systematically increasing exposure to high-upside opportunities.

13.3 Innovation Portfolios & Optionality

Innovation is inherently uncertain. Every new idea, technology, or business model carries unknown risks, and outcomes are often non-linear and widely dispersed. Just as financial portfolios diversify capital across assets, entrepreneurs can create **innovation portfolios** collections of projects, experiments, and strategic initiatives designed to maximize upside while limiting downside. Coupled with **optionality**, this approach allows founders to thrive in uncertainty, systematically capturing opportunities that others might miss.

The Concept of Innovation Portfolios

An innovation portfolio is a deliberately structured set of initiatives that balances risk, reward, and learning potential. Instead of placing all bets on a single idea, entrepreneurs distribute effort, resources, and attention across multiple experiments or projects:

- **High-risk, high-reward projects:** Small initiatives with the potential to scale dramatically if successful.
- **Moderate-risk experiments:** Initiatives with measurable upside and manageable downside that test core assumptions about customers, technology, or market fit.
- **Low-risk sustaining innovations:** Incremental improvements that provide stable feedback and maintain current business operations.

This layered approach mirrors a probabilistic strategy: a few big wins can dominate long-term outcomes, while smaller initiatives provide continuous learning and optionality.

Optionality as a Strategic Tool

Optionality is the ability to act or pivot when opportunities arise, without being locked into a single path. In innovation, optionality is created when projects are designed to:

- Require minimal upfront investment relative to potential payoff.
- Preserve the flexibility to scale, pivot, or abandon based on new information.
- Allow sequential decision-making, where each stage informs the next.

By embedding optionality into an innovation portfolio, founders convert uncertainty into strategic advantage. The key is not to predict which project will succeed, but to ensure that success in any initiative has the potential to produce outsized returns while limiting irreversible losses.

Designing an Innovation Portfolio

1. **Map opportunities:** List all possible experiments, products, or initiatives. Consider market trends, emerging technologies, and unmet customer needs.
2. **Assess expected value and variance:** Estimate upside, downside, and likelihood of success for each opportunity. Focus on high-edge bets.
3. **Allocate resources strategically:** Diversify effort across multiple projects according to expected value and risk tolerance. Ensure no single failure jeopardizes the overall portfolio.
4. **Preserve optionality:** Design projects to allow pivots, scaling, or early exit if conditions change. Use modular structures, staged funding, or iterative development.
5. **Implement feedback loops:** Continuously measure outcomes, update assumptions, and reallocate resources to maximize learning and long-term upside.

Case Examples

- **Tech startups:** Companies like Google and Amazon maintain multiple initiatives simultaneously, from core revenue-generating products to speculative moonshots, ensuring exposure to high-variance successes while mitigating risk.
- **Venture capital approach:** VCs invest small amounts in many startups, knowing most will fail but a few will deliver outsized returns essentially managing an innovation portfolio with optionality.
- **Corporate innovation:** Firms like 3M and Tesla encourage small, exploratory projects that can be rapidly scaled if early results are promising, embedding optionality in their R&D pipelines.

Psychological and Strategic Advantages

- **Reduces fear of failure:** Small, diversified bets prevent catastrophic outcomes and allow calculated risk-taking.
- **Enhances learning:** Multiple parallel experiments accelerate feedback, revealing insights that inform future decisions.
- **Maximizes optionality:** By maintaining flexibility, entrepreneurs can capitalize on unexpected opportunities or pivot in response to market shifts.
- **Encourages long-term thinking:** Portfolios reduce overreliance on short-term successes, allowing cumulative probabilistic advantages to compound over time.

Implementing Probabilistic Thinking in Innovation Portfolios

To fully leverage the power of portfolios and optionality, integrate probabilistic reasoning:

- **Estimate probabilities of success:** Assign likelihoods to each initiative and update them as new information emerges.
- **Focus on expected value:** Prioritize initiatives where the potential payoff multiplied by probability exceeds risk exposure.
- **Anticipate tail events:** Include optionality for extreme market shifts, technological breakthroughs, or competitor moves.
- **Iterate continuously:** Treat each experiment as a Bayesian update, adjusting future bets and reallocating resources dynamically.

Key Takeaways

- Innovation portfolios spread risk across multiple initiatives while preserving the potential for outsized success.
- Optionality allows entrepreneurs to pivot, scale, or abandon projects based on emerging data, turning uncertainty into a competitive advantage.
- Probabilistic thinking ensures resources are allocated efficiently, balancing risk, reward, and learning.

- Over time, disciplined use of portfolios and optionality compounds both knowledge and opportunity, increasing the likelihood of transformative outcomes.

By combining innovation portfolios with optionality, entrepreneurs design systems that thrive under uncertainty. Instead of betting everything on a single idea, they create structured, probabilistic experiments where learning compounds, risk is managed, and opportunities for outsized impact multiply. In the high-variance world of startups, this approach transforms volatility and unpredictability into strategic levers for growth, resilience, and long-term success.

Chapter 14

Problem-Solving Creativity

Innovation and problem-solving thrive at the intersection of structured reasoning and creative exploration. In a world filled with uncertainty and complex challenges, the ability to approach problems probabilistically considering multiple possibilities, embracing ambiguity, and leveraging creativity is a critical advantage. This chapter explores how probabilistic thinking enhances problem-solving, the dynamics between divergent and convergent thinking, and how to harness serendipity and creative probability to generate transformative solutions.

14.1 Divergent vs. Convergent Thinking

At the heart of creative problem-solving lies the interplay between two fundamentally different modes of thought: **divergent thinking** and **convergent thinking**. Understanding and mastering these cognitive modes is essential for anyone looking to navigate complex problems, innovate, and make smarter decisions under uncertainty.

Divergent Thinking: Generating Possibilities

Divergent thinking is the process of exploring multiple ideas, pathways, or solutions without immediate judgment. It emphasizes creativity, imagination, and the expansion of possibilities. In probabilistic problem-solving, divergent thinking is crucial because it multiplies the potential pathways to success, increasing the likelihood of finding high-impact solutions.

Core Principles of Divergent Thinking

- **Quantity over quality:** At the early stage of idea generation, the more options you create, the higher the chance that one of them is exceptional. Even seemingly trivial ideas can spark breakthroughs when combined or refined.
- **Suspension of judgment:** Avoid evaluating or rejecting ideas prematurely. Every idea, no matter how unconventional, has potential informational or combinatorial value.
- **Associative thinking:** Connect disparate concepts, disciplines, or experiences to generate novel solutions. Many innovations emerge at the intersection of unrelated domains.
- **Exploring extremes:** Consider radical or extreme possibilities. In high-variance systems, outlier ideas can produce outsized returns, while conventional solutions may only yield incremental gains.

Practical Techniques for Divergent Thinking

- **Brainstorming sessions:** Encourage participants to generate as many ideas as possible within a set timeframe, deferring evaluation until later.
- **Mind mapping:** Visualize relationships between concepts to uncover connections that are not immediately obvious.
- **SCAMPER method:** Systematically explore ways to Substitute, Combine, Adapt, Modify, Put to another use, Eliminate, or Reverse existing ideas.
- **Random input stimulation:** Introduce unrelated stimuli, such as images, words, or scenarios, to spark creative associations.

Convergent Thinking: Narrowing and Refining

While divergent thinking generates possibilities, convergent thinking evaluates, filters, and synthesizes these options into actionable solutions. It is analytical, structured, and goal-oriented, turning creativity into practical results.

Core Principles of Convergent Thinking

- **Critical evaluation:** Examine each idea for feasibility, impact, cost, and alignment with objectives.
- **Prioritization:** Identify high-expected-value options ideas where potential payoff outweighs risk exposure.

- **Integration:** Combine complementary ideas into cohesive solutions that leverage strengths and mitigate weaknesses.
- **Iterative refinement:** Use feedback loops to continuously improve selected ideas, incorporating learning from experiments or real-world testing.

Techniques for Effective Convergent Thinking

- **Decision matrices:** Score and rank ideas based on criteria such as feasibility, potential impact, and alignment with strategic goals.
- **Prototyping and testing:** Convert ideas into minimum viable solutions to gather data and validate assumptions.
- **Scenario analysis:** Explore potential outcomes for each option under different conditions, updating probabilities as new information emerges.
- **Cost-benefit evaluation:** Assess resource allocation and opportunity cost to focus on initiatives with the highest expected value.

The Probabilistic Advantage of Balancing Divergence and Convergence

In uncertain environments, neither divergent nor convergent thinking alone is sufficient. Divergence without convergence leads to endless ideation with no actionable results. Convergence without divergence stifles creativity and limits the probability of discovering high-impact solutions. By alternating between these modes:

- **Increase probabilistic coverage:** More ideas generated in divergence increase the likelihood that at least one path leads to a breakthrough.
- **Refine probabilistic bets:** Convergent analysis filters ideas based on expected value, allowing resources to focus on the highest potential outcomes.
- **Enhance optionality:** Generating multiple options and refining the most promising ones preserves flexibility to pivot or scale as new information emerges.

Case Examples and Applications

- **Entrepreneurship:** Startups often brainstorm dozens of product ideas (divergent thinking) before selecting the most viable option to develop and launch (convergent thinking).
- **Scientific research:** Researchers generate multiple hypotheses or experimental approaches, then test and refine them systematically to identify robust conclusions.
- **Corporate strategy:** Organizations explore multiple market entry strategies or business models before committing resources to the most promising pathway.
- **Creative arts:** Writers, designers, and innovators produce numerous drafts or concepts before curating and refining the final product.

Key Takeaways

- Divergent thinking expands the solution space, multiplying opportunities in uncertain, high-variance environments.
- Convergent thinking narrows options, focusing resources on high-expected-value paths.
- Alternating between divergence and convergence allows probabilistic optimization: exploring many possibilities while making disciplined, informed decisions.
- Mastery of these modes enhances creativity, resilience, and strategic flexibility, turning uncertainty into a source of competitive advantage.

By consciously practicing divergent and convergent thinking, individuals and organizations create a structured approach to creativity and problem-solving. This framework transforms randomness and uncertainty into opportunity, enabling the discovery of high-impact solutions while minimizing wasted effort and resources.

14.2 Exploring Multiple Solution Pathways

Complex problems rarely have a single, clear-cut solution. In uncertain, high-variance environments, relying on one approach is risky; failure in that single pathway can be catastrophic. Instead, probabilistic problem-solving emphasizes exploring multiple solution pathways simultaneously, evaluating their likelihood of success, and maintaining flexibility to pivot as new information emerges. By thinking in terms of options rather than certainties, we increase the chances of discovering high-impact solutions while mitigating downside risk.

The Logic Behind Multiple Pathways

When faced with uncertainty, each potential solution represents a "bet" with its own probability distribution of outcomes. Some solutions carry high upside but low probability, while others offer moderate returns with higher likelihood. By pursuing multiple pathways in parallel, we diversify our bets and create optionality:

- If one pathway fails, others may succeed, preventing total loss.
- Each pathway generates valuable feedback, even if it doesn't lead to immediate success.
- Maintaining multiple avenues increases the overall expected value of the problem-solving process.

This approach mirrors portfolio management in finance, where diversification reduces risk while retaining exposure to high-return opportunities. In creative and strategic problem-solving, multiple solution pathways serve the same function: they turn uncertainty into a structured probabilistic advantage.

Techniques for Exploring Multiple Pathways

Scenario Planning Map different plausible futures and design strategies for each. By envisioning multiple potential outcomes, decision-makers can preemptively prepare solutions that perform well across a variety of conditions. Scenario planning encourages flexibility and reduces the risk of being blindsided by unexpected developments.

Parallel Experimentation Test several solutions simultaneously on a small scale before committing full resources. For example, a startup might run multiple marketing campaigns, prototype several product features, or explore alternative business models in parallel. This experimentation increases learning speed and provides probabilistic insight into which options are likely to succeed.

Hypothesis Diversification Treat each solution pathway as a testable hypothesis. Explicitly define assumptions, success metrics, and potential risks for each path. This ensures that experimentation is structured, measurable, and capable of generating actionable data.

Iterative Feedback Loops Use real-time feedback to update beliefs and probabilities. If evidence suggests a solution is unlikely to succeed, pivot or reallocate resources to higher-potential pathways. Iterative loops prevent sunk-cost fallacies and encourage adaptive, evidence-based decision-making.

The Psychological Benefits

Exploring multiple pathways not only improves strategic outcomes but also enhances cognitive resilience:

- **Reduces fear of failure:** Knowing that alternatives exist lowers the stakes of any single decision, encouraging experimentation.
- **Encourages creativity:** Multiple options stimulate divergent thinking and open new avenues for innovation.
- **Supports learning:** Even failed paths provide data, refining probability estimates and informing future decisions.
- **Enhances confidence:** Maintaining multiple pathways allows decision-makers to act decisively, knowing they are not locked into a single uncertain route.

Real-World Applications

- **Entrepreneurship:** A founder might test multiple product concepts simultaneously in different market segments before scaling the most promising one.
- **Scientific research:** Researchers often explore various experimental methodologies to validate a hypothesis, rather than relying on a single experimental design.
- **Corporate strategy:** Companies may explore multiple market entry strategies, partnerships, or technological approaches to hedge against uncertainty.
- **Personal decision-making:** Individuals can apply this mindset by pursuing multiple career or learning opportunities in parallel, increasing the probability of long-term success.

Key Takeaways

- Uncertainty demands flexibility: single-path solutions are fragile in complex systems.
- Multiple solution pathways diversify probabilistic bets, increasing the likelihood of discovering high-impact outcomes.
- Structured experimentation, scenario planning, and iterative feedback loops turn uncertainty into a learning and advantage-generating system.
- Maintaining optionality keeping alternative solutions viable enhances both strategic and psychological resilience.

By consciously exploring multiple solution pathways, problem-solvers shift from reactive decision-making to proactive probabilistic strategy. Each pathway functions as an experiment, generating insight, reducing risk, and preserving optionality. Over time, this approach compounds both knowledge and opportunity, transforming uncertainty from a threat into a source of innovation and competitive advantage.

14.3 Serendipity and Creative Probability

Many of history's most transformative discoveries and innovations have arisen not through meticulous planning alone, but through chance encounters, unexpected insights, or fortunate accidents. This phenomenon is known as **serendipity** the art of finding valuable things not sought for. While serendipity may seem purely random, probabilistic thinking allows us to *increase the likelihood of serendipitous events* and leverage them systematically to generate creative breakthroughs.

Understanding Serendipity as a Probabilistic System

Serendipity is not mere luck it is a function of exposure, preparation, and optionality. In probabilistic terms, serendipity occurs when:

- **Multiple potential pathways exist:** The more diverse ideas, projects, and experiments one engages with, the higher the probability of encountering unexpected connections.
- **Chance events intersect with preparedness:** Being knowledgeable, attentive, and open-minded allows one to recognize the value of unexpected observations.

- **Optionality is maintained:** Flexible strategies, parallel experiments, and multiple pathways preserve the ability to act on unexpected opportunities when they arise.

In short, serendipity can be cultivated by intentionally creating an environment where randomness can yield meaningful outcomes.

Techniques to Maximize Serendipitous Discovery

Expanding Exposure Engage with diverse people, disciplines, and environments. Cross-pollination of ideas across fields often produces insights that would not emerge within a single domain. Attending conferences, reading broadly, collaborating across industries, and exploring unfamiliar domains increases the number of potential "collision points" for novel ideas.

Maintaining Optionality Treat multiple projects or ideas as live experiments. Just as investors maintain a portfolio of bets, creative thinkers maintain a portfolio of exploratory initiatives. Optionality ensures that when unexpected opportunities arise, you have the freedom to act without being overcommitted to a single path.

Systematic Observation and Documentation Keep a record of insights, observations, and experiments even those that seem irrelevant. Many innovations emerge from recombining previously unrelated ideas. Tools such as idea journals, mind maps, or digital knowledge systems can capture these serendipitous sparks for future use.

Creating Random Encounters Introduce controlled randomness into your workflow. This could include brainstorming with new collaborators, exploring different industries, or exposing yourself to unfamiliar ideas. Random exposure increases the probability of encountering valuable yet unplanned information.

The Role of Probabilistic Thinking

Serendipity is inherently probabilistic: not every encounter or experiment will yield value. By thinking in terms of probabilities, we can:

- **Quantify exposure:** Recognize that increasing the number of ideas, experiments, or interactions raises the chance of breakthrough outcomes.
- **Prioritize high-probability actions:** Focus on actions that generate the greatest number of potential "collision points" with minimal cost.

- **Balance risk and reward:** Allocate time and resources to exploratory initiatives that have asymmetric upside, even if the probability of immediate success is low.

This approach turns random chance into a structured, opportunity maximizing system.

Case Examples of Serendipity

- **Scientific discovery:** Alexander Fleming's discovery of penicillin was a result of noticing an unexpected mold growth contaminating a bacterial culture. His awareness and preparation allowed him to recognize its value.
- **Entrepreneurship:** Many startup pivots arise from chance insights about customer behavior or market gaps discovered while exploring multiple initiatives.
- **Art and design:** Artists and designers often find inspiration in unrelated fields, leading to innovative combinations and unique creations.
- **Everyday problem-solving:** Casual conversations, reading unrelated articles, or observing patterns in nature can trigger ideas that solve ongoing challenges in unexpected ways.

Key Takeaways

- Serendipity is not pure luck it can be cultivated through exposure, optionality, and preparedness.
- The probability of creative breakthroughs increases with the number of ideas, experiments, and interactions.
- Maintaining flexible pathways and documenting observations allows unexpected insights to be recognized and acted upon.
- Controlled randomness, cross-domain learning, and a probabilistic mindset transform uncertainty into a source of opportunity.

By intentionally designing environments and systems that maximize the likelihood of serendipitous events, problem-solvers and innovators can convert randomness into a strategic asset. The probabilistic thinker does not wait for luck she increases the odds that chance will work in her favor, systematically creating opportunities for discovery, creativity, and high-impact solutions.

Chapter 15

Negotiation Risk Management

Negotiation and risk management are two sides of the same coin: both involve making decisions under uncertainty, managing probabilities, and optimizing outcomes in environments where information is imperfect and stakes are high. Whether in business deals, strategic partnerships, or personal agreements, the ability to navigate uncertainty with a probabilistic mindset can mean the difference between success and failure.

Traditional negotiation often relies on fixed positions, assumptions of certainty, or zero-sum thinking. However, in complex, dynamic situations, this deterministic approach is fragile. Probabilistic negotiation embraces uncertainty, considers multiple potential outcomes, and evaluates the likelihood of each scenario. By integrating risk management principles, negotiators can protect themselves from downside exposure while simultaneously positioning themselves to capture asymmetric gains.

15.1 Negotiating Under Uncertainty

Negotiation is rarely a simple exchange of fixed offers and counteroffers. In most real-world scenarios, information is incomplete, outcomes are probabilistic, and the future is unpredictable. Traditional negotiation tactics, which assume certainty and linear outcomes, often fail in these complex environments. A probabilistic mindset, however, transforms negotiation into a structured process that balances risk, opportunity, and strategic thinking under uncertainty.

The Nature of Uncertainty in Negotiation

Uncertainty arises in negotiation from multiple sources:

- **Incomplete information:** You rarely know the other party's priorities, constraints, or thresholds.
- **Dynamic contexts:** External factors such as market conditions, regulations, or stakeholder pressures can change during the negotiation.
- **Human behavior:** Opponents may act unpredictably, strategically misrepresent information, or adapt in response to your moves.

Recognizing these uncertainties is the first step in probabilistic negotiation. Instead of pretending certainty exists, skilled negotiators map the range of possible outcomes and assign relative probabilities to each. This allows them to make decisions that maximize expected value while mitigating downside risk.

Probabilistic Decision-Making in Negotiation

A probabilistic approach to negotiation involves evaluating offers, concessions, and strategies in terms of expected outcomes rather than absolute values. For example:

- Consider not just the most likely outcome, but also the best-case and worst-case scenarios.
- Assign probabilities to different outcomes based on available information, past patterns, or strategic reasoning.
- Make concessions and commitments proportional to the expected value, not to the apparent certainty of success.

By quantifying uncertainty and explicitly considering probabilities, negotiators can identify options that offer asymmetric upside with limited downside.

Strategies for Negotiating Under Uncertainty

Prepare Multiple Scenarios Before entering negotiations, develop a set of plausible scenarios for how the discussion might unfold. For each scenario, outline potential offers, counteroffers, and acceptable concessions. This preparation allows you to respond adaptively as the negotiation evolves, rather than being trapped by unexpected moves.

Establish Flexible Anchors Anchoring is a common negotiation tactic, but rigid anchors can be dangerous under uncertainty. Instead, use flexible anchors that set aspirational goals while preserving room for adjustment as new information emerges.

Incremental Commitments Avoid locking into large, irreversible commitments early in the negotiation. Break agreements into smaller, contingent steps that can be adapted as circumstances change. This approach preserves optionality and limits exposure to unfavorable outcomes.

Information Gathering and Signaling Actively seek information about the other party's preferences and constraints, while carefully managing what you reveal. Subtle signals, probing questions, and testing responses can provide probabilistic insight into likely outcomes without overcommitting.

Contingent Agreements Where outcomes are highly uncertain, consider agreements that include contingencies or conditional clauses. For example, performance-based contracts or milestone-based payments allow both parties to share risk while maintaining incentives for success.

Psychological Advantages of Probabilistic Negotiation

Approaching negotiation probabilistically also confers significant psychological benefits:

- **Reduces stress and fear of failure:** Understanding that outcomes are uncertain allows negotiators to act with confidence without overestimating the consequences of a single misstep.
- **Encourages creativity:** Considering multiple pathways and probabilistic outcomes inspires alternative solutions, trade-offs, and novel value-creation approaches.
- **Enhances adaptability:** Probabilistic thinking prepares negotiators to pivot in response to new information or unexpected moves.

Case Example: Business Negotiation Under Uncertainty

Imagine a company negotiating a strategic partnership with a supplier. Key uncertainties include future market demand, competitor actions, and regulatory changes. A deterministic approach might focus solely on price, potentially ignoring flexibility or long-term options. A probabilistic approach, in contrast, would:

- Map potential future market scenarios (e.g., high demand, moderate demand, low demand) and assign probabilities.
- Structure the contract with contingent pricing, volume commitments, and exit clauses aligned to each scenario.
- Keep alternative suppliers and partnerships as optionality in case initial negotiations fail.
- Make incremental commitments while continuously updating beliefs based on supplier signals and market developments.

This approach turns uncertainty into a strategic advantage, allowing the company to maximize expected value while mitigating downside risk.

Key Takeaways

- Uncertainty is inherent in negotiation; ignoring it is a recipe for failure.
- A probabilistic mindset allows you to evaluate multiple outcomes, make expected-value-driven decisions, and preserve optionality.
- Strategies like scenario planning, incremental commitments, and contingent agreements increase flexibility and reduce exposure to risk.
- Probabilistic negotiation enhances adaptability, creativity, and confidence, transforming uncertainty from a liability into a competitive advantage.

By integrating probabilistic thinking into negotiation, you no longer need to rely solely on power, persuasion, or luck. Instead, you approach discussions as a system of probabilities, optional pathways, and structured decisions turning the inherent uncertainty of negotiation into a source of strategic opportunity.

15.2 Game Theory in Real-World Scenarios

Negotiation and strategic decision-making rarely occur in isolation. Every action you take can influence, and be influenced by, the decisions of others. This interdependence is the essence of **game theory**, a framework for analyzing situations where multiple actors interact under conditions of strategic uncertainty. By understanding game theory, you can anticipate the behavior of counterparts, identify optimal strategies, and structure negotiations and decisions to maximize expected outcomes.

Fundamentals of Game Theory

Game theory provides a probabilistic lens through which to evaluate strategic interactions. Its core concepts include:

- **Players:** The decision-makers involved in the interaction. In negotiation, this could be yourself, the counterparty, and even external stakeholders.
- **Strategies:** The set of possible actions each player can take. A strategy may involve an initial offer, a counterproposal, or a contingent move based on new information.
- **Payoffs:** The outcomes associated with each combination of strategies, usually expressed in terms of value, utility, or probability-weighted gains and losses.
- **Equilibrium:** A state in which no player can improve their outcome by unilaterally changing their strategy, often referred to as the Nash equilibrium.

In practical negotiation, you rarely calculate precise numerical payoffs. Instead, you use probabilistic reasoning to anticipate likely behaviors, understand incentives, and position yourself for asymmetric advantage.

Common Game-Theoretic Scenarios

The Prisoner's Dilemma Two parties may benefit from cooperation, but the incentive to defect for short-term gain can lead both to suboptimal outcomes. In business, this occurs when competitors or partners have conflicting incentives. Recognizing this, you can structure agreements, incentives, or reputational mechanisms to align long-term interests and reduce the risk of defection.

The Ultimatum Game One party proposes a division of resources, and the other can accept or reject it. Rejection results in no payoff for either party. This highlights the importance of fairness, perceived value, and behavioral expectations in negotiation. Probabilistic thinking helps you anticipate the likelihood of acceptance based on context, culture, and the counterpart's incentives.

The Stag Hunt This game illustrates the tension between safety and potential high reward. Players may choose a safe, moderate payoff or coordinate for a higher payoff that requires trust and cooperation. In negotiation, this parallels situations where joint ventures or collaborative deals can yield outsized value if both parties commit, but failure to coordinate leads to smaller gains.

Sequential Moves and Signaling Many real-world interactions are sequential rather than simultaneous. Early actions can signal intent, strength, or preference to other parties, influencing their subsequent choices. By anticipating responses and signaling strategically, you can manipulate the probabilities of favorable outcomes.

Applying Game Theory in Probabilistic Negotiation

Game theory enhances negotiation by:

- **Anticipating counterparty behavior:** Understanding incentives and potential strategies allows you to predict likely responses and avoid surprises.
- **Optimizing your moves:** Structuring offers, concessions, or commitments to maximize expected value based on the probable strategies of others.
- **Creating asymmetric advantage:** By identifying situations where you have more information, flexibility, or resources, you can tilt outcomes in your favor.
- **Mitigating risk:** Recognizing the interdependence of actions helps you avoid strategies that could backfire if the other party acts unpredictably.

Case Example: Negotiating a Joint Venture

Consider two companies negotiating a joint venture in a new market. Both parties have multiple strategies:

- **Company A:** Aggressively pursue a controlling stake or accept a minority share to minimize risk.
- **Company B:** Offer flexible revenue sharing, insist on equal control, or walk away to pursue other partners.

Game-theoretic thinking would involve:

- Mapping the payoff matrix for each strategy combination.
- Evaluating the probabilities of acceptance, rejection, or counteroffers.
- Considering signaling actions, such as public announcements, pilot projects, or early investments, to influence the other party's strategy.
- Designing contingent agreements that align incentives, protect against downside, and maximize expected value for both sides.

By applying probabilistic reasoning within a game-theoretic framework, negotiators can transform a complex, uncertain interaction into a structured process that optimizes outcomes.

Key Takeaways

- Game theory provides a framework for understanding strategic interactions under uncertainty.
- Most negotiations are not zero-sum; anticipating behavior and aligning incentives can create mutually beneficial outcomes.
- Probabilistic thinking complements game theory by helping you assign likelihoods, evaluate risk, and focus on expected value.
- Structured approaches such as payoff matrices, signaling, and contingency planning increase strategic flexibility and reduce vulnerability to surprises.

In essence, game theory equips negotiators with a mental model to anticipate, influence, and respond to the behavior of others. When combined with probabilistic thinking, it transforms uncertainty from a source of fear into a source of strategic advantage, allowing negotiators to act decisively and optimize outcomes in complex, dynamic environments.

15.3 Hedging Against Downside

In negotiation and strategic decision-making, the most skilled players understand that protecting themselves from catastrophic loss is as important as pursuing upside. This is the essence of **hedging against downside** structuring decisions, agreements, and strategies so that negative outcomes are limited, even under high uncertainty. Hedging does not eliminate risk, but it transforms unpredictable environments into systems where losses are manageable and potential gains remain attractive.

The Concept of Downside Protection

Downside protection is a central principle in both finance and negotiation. It involves taking deliberate steps to limit the impact of adverse outcomes. Key principles include:

- **Optionality:** Maintain the ability to pivot or abandon a strategy if circumstances change.
- **Contingent agreements:** Structure deals with conditions or milestones that mitigate exposure to negative outcomes.

- **Diversification of strategies:** Spread risk across multiple pathways to avoid overexposure to any single outcome.
- **Small, reversible commitments:** Make incremental decisions that preserve flexibility and limit the potential for irreversible loss.

In essence, hedging is about designing negotiations and strategies so that even low-probability negative events cannot derail long-term objectives.

Techniques for Hedging in Negotiation

Contingent Clauses Include clauses in agreements that adjust obligations based on future events. For example, performance-based contracts, milestone payments, or exit options ensure that commitments scale appropriately with outcomes, reducing the risk of total loss.

Incremental Commitment Avoid front-loading decisions or investments. By breaking agreements into phased steps, negotiators retain the ability to reassess and redirect resources as new information emerges.

Diversification of Options Maintain multiple potential partnerships, suppliers, or strategies. If one path fails, alternative avenues preserve value and reduce the probability of catastrophic failure.

Risk-Sharing Structures Distribute risk between parties to align incentives. For example, joint ventures, shared investments, or co-development agreements allow each party to benefit from upside while limiting exposure to downside.

Insurance and Guarantees Where applicable, financial or contractual instruments can provide explicit protection against adverse outcomes. These include guarantees, performance bonds, or hedging instruments in financial contexts.

Psychological and Strategic Benefits

Hedging against downside offers both cognitive and strategic advantages:

- **Reduces fear and paralysis:** Knowing that negative outcomes are bounded allows negotiators to act decisively.
- **Encourages calculated risk-taking:** When potential losses are limited, negotiators can pursue high-upside opportunities without reckless exposure.

- **Preserves long-term relationships:** Risk-sharing and contingency planning prevent disputes and foster trust between parties.
- **Supports probabilistic thinking:** Hedging is a tangible application of expected-value reasoning, aligning actions with the likelihood and impact of various outcomes.

Case Example: Protecting Against Contract Risk

Consider a company negotiating a multi-year supply agreement with a new vendor. The future is uncertain: market demand may fluctuate, and the vendor's performance is untested. A hedged approach would involve:

- Structuring the contract in phases with performance-based milestones.
- Maintaining alternative suppliers as backup options.
- Including clauses that allow adjustment of quantities or pricing if demand changes.
- Sharing risk through co-investment in inventory or technology to align incentives.

This structure limits downside exposure while preserving the potential for gains if the partnership succeeds, exemplifying how hedging transforms uncertainty into strategic advantage.

Key Takeaways

- Downside risk is inevitable in negotiation, but it can be managed through careful planning and probabilistic reasoning.
- Hedging techniques such as optionality, contingent clauses, incremental commitments, and diversification protect against catastrophic outcomes.
- Strategically limiting losses empowers negotiators to pursue high-upside opportunities without fear, enhancing both flexibility and confidence.
- Hedging is a practical application of probabilistic thinking, turning uncertainty from a threat into a source of competitive advantage.

By systematically hedging against downside, negotiators and decision-makers ensure that uncertainty does not become a liability. Instead, it becomes a manageable component of a probabilistic strategy, allowing calculated risk-taking, adaptive decision-making, and sustainable value creation.

Part IV

Mastery Long-Term Perspective

Chapter 16

Probabilistic Resilience

Life is inherently uncertain. No matter how much we plan, unexpected challenges, shocks, and disruptions are inevitable. The key to long-term success, fulfillment, and stability is not avoiding uncertainty, but building the ability to **thrive within it**. This ability is what we call **probabilistic resilience** the capacity to absorb shocks, adapt to stress, and leverage randomness to your advantage.

Traditional notions of resilience focus on recovery bouncing back to a previous state after a setback. Probabilistic resilience goes further. It integrates principles of anti-fragility, stress adaptation, and probabilistic thinking to create systems whether in your career, relationships, finances, or personal habits that not only withstand volatility but improve in response to it.

16.1 Anti-fragility and Stress Adaptation

Resilience is often thought of as the ability to recover from setbacks, to "bounce back" after adversity. While valuable, this notion only describes systems that maintain stability under stress. **Anti-fragility**, a concept popularized by Nassim Nicholas Taleb, goes beyond resilience: it describes systems that actually *improve* when exposed to stress, volatility, and uncertainty. Anti-fragile systems do not merely survive shocks they learn, adapt, and grow stronger as a result.

Understanding Anti-Fragility

Anti-fragility differs from three related concepts:

- **Fragile:** Easily broken or disrupted by volatility or stress. A fragile system performs well under calm conditions but fails catastrophically under pressure.

- **Robust/Resilient:** Withstands shocks and maintains its function but does not improve from stress. It survives volatility but does not gain from it.
- **Anti-fragile:** Benefits from volatility, randomness, and stress. The system learns, adapts, and becomes stronger when challenged.

For individuals, organizations, and life systems, anti-fragility means creating environments and routines where controlled exposure to stress and variability generates growth, learning, and long-term advantage.

The Role of Stress Adaptation

Stress adaptation is the mechanism through which anti-fragility operates. Just as muscles grow stronger when subjected to controlled resistance, personal and systemic resilience grows when challenges are approached intentionally:

- **Hormesis in biology:** Small doses of stress like exercise, intermittent fasting, or cold exposure trigger adaptive responses that strengthen the body.
- **Cognitive stress:** Learning to solve complex problems, confront uncertainty, or make probabilistic decisions exercises the mind's capacity to handle volatility.
- **Social and emotional stress:** Navigating difficult interpersonal situations, facing criticism, and resolving conflicts builds emotional intelligence and relational resilience.

By intentionally exposing yourself to manageable stressors, you train both mind and body to adapt, making you more capable of handling larger, unpredictable shocks.

Principles of Anti-Fragile Systems

To cultivate anti-fragility, systems whether personal, financial, or organizational should follow these principles:

- **Small, frequent stressors:** Expose the system to manageable challenges regularly rather than one overwhelming shock. This reduces fragility while promoting adaptation.
- **Redundancy and optionality:** Multiple pathways, backup plans, and flexible strategies allow the system to absorb failures and exploit opportunities.

- **Decentralization:** Distributed systems are less vulnerable to single points of failure. Diversity and independence create robustness and anti-fragility.
- **Feedback loops:** Regular feedback allows rapid learning and adjustment. Mistakes and failures become data points for system improvement.
- **Skin in the game:** Personal accountability and direct exposure to consequences encourage careful, adaptive decision-making. Those insulated from risk rarely develop anti-fragile behaviors.

Applications in Personal Life and Career

Anti-fragility is not limited to abstract systems it can be applied directly to individual growth:

- **Career development:** Pursue projects and roles that stretch your skills and expose you to uncertainty. Failures in low-stakes environments teach lessons that compound into future advantage.
- **Financial decisions:** Maintain optionality in investments, diversify, and take calculated asymmetric risks where small losses are acceptable but upside is substantial.
- **Learning and skill-building:** Constantly challenge yourself to learn new domains, solve novel problems, and embrace uncertainty as a training ground for cognitive resilience.
- **Health and habits:** Introduce controlled stressors like intermittent fasting, cold showers, or challenging workouts to improve physical and mental robustness.

Case Example: Anti-Fragile Career Strategy

Consider a professional entering a rapidly changing industry, such as AI or fintech. A fragile approach would be to specialize narrowly and avoid risk, leaving them vulnerable to disruption. A robust approach would maintain current skills and avoid change, surviving but not improving. An anti-fragile strategy involves:

- Taking on challenging projects that require learning new technologies.
- Building a diverse network of mentors and collaborators to increase optionality.

- Accepting small, calculated career risks, such as launching a side project or pivoting roles.
- Using failures and feedback as a source of learning, allowing each setback to strengthen capability.

This approach not only prepares the individual for future shocks but leverages uncertainty as a source of growth, positioning them to thrive in volatile environments.

Key Takeaways

- Anti-fragility is the ability to benefit from stress, volatility, and randomness, going beyond mere resilience.
- Stress adaptation, through controlled exposure to challenges, strengthens both mind and body.
- Principles such as optionality, redundancy, feedback, decentralization, and skin in the game cultivate anti-fragile systems.
- Applying anti-fragility to careers, learning, health, and finances allows you to turn uncertainty into a source of advantage rather than vulnerability.

By understanding and applying anti-fragility, you can transform challenges, failures, and unpredictable events into engines of growth. Probabilistic resilience is not about avoiding stress it is about using stress intelligently to adapt, improve, and thrive under uncertainty.

16.2 Thriving Under Uncertainty

Uncertainty is a constant in life markets fluctuate, technology evolves, relationships shift, and health can change unexpectedly. While many people instinctively resist uncertainty, the truly successful learn to **thrive within it**. Thriving under uncertainty is not about eliminating risk or predicting the future perfectly; it is about designing systems, habits, and mental models that allow you to leverage volatility, capitalize on opportunities, and grow stronger as unpredictability unfolds.

The Mindset of Thriving

Thriving under uncertainty begins with a probabilistic mindset:

- **Focus on expected value, not certainty:** Decisions should be evaluated based on probable outcomes and their associated impact rather than on guaranteed results.
- **Embrace optionality:** Keep multiple paths open so that unexpected changes create new opportunities rather than dead ends.
- **Detach from outcomes:** Measure success by the quality of decisions and process rather than immediate results. This reduces emotional volatility and preserves clarity under stress.
- **See randomness as opportunity:** Unexpected events can be asymmetric; the right strategy turns small inputs into outsized gains when chance favors your preparation.

This mindset allows individuals to perceive uncertainty not as a threat but as a dynamic environment in which they can exert influence and capture value.

Strategies for Thriving Under Uncertainty

Build Redundant and Flexible Systems Whether in finance, career, or health, redundancy reduces fragility and provides the freedom to act on emerging opportunities. For example, maintaining multiple income streams or diverse skill sets ensures that setbacks in one area do not derail overall progress.

Adopt an Iterative, Experimental Approach Treat decisions as experiments. Small bets with measurable feedback allow you to test hypotheses, learn rapidly, and adapt strategies. Iteration transforms uncertainty into a learning engine.

Focus on What You Can Control While the world is unpredictable, your actions, preparation, and response mechanisms are controllable. By maximizing influence over controllable variables, you reduce exposure to harmful randomness.

Develop Cognitive Flexibility Cognitive flexibility enables quick adjustment to changing conditions. This includes re-evaluating assumptions, considering alternative scenarios, and thinking probabilistically about potential outcomes.

Exploit Asymmetry Look for situations where the potential upside greatly exceeds the potential downside. Even under uncertainty, asymmetric opportunities create positive expected value while minimizing exposure to catastrophic loss.

Psychological Adaptations

Thriving under uncertainty also requires emotional and psychological resilience:

- **Detach ego from outcomes:** Avoid tying self-worth to immediate success or failure. This encourages rational decisions under stress.
- **Cultivate patience:** Many high-probability advantages only manifest over time. Resisting impulsive reactions allows optionality to compound.
- **Accept impermanence:** Recognize that change is constant. Embracing transience reduces fear and promotes adaptability.
- **Normalize volatility:** Frequent exposure to controlled uncertainty builds tolerance, making unpredictable shocks less destabilizing psychologically.

Case Example: Thriving in a Volatile Market

Consider an entrepreneur in a rapidly evolving technology sector. The environment is highly unpredictable: consumer preferences shift, competitors innovate, and regulations change. To thrive:

- They diversify products and markets to maintain optionality.
- Small-scale experiments test features and marketing strategies before scaling.
- Financial buffers and contingency plans mitigate the impact of negative events.
- Every failure is treated as a learning opportunity, refining strategy and improving decision-making for the future.

Rather than fearing volatility, the entrepreneur leverages it, using uncertainty as a source of insight and competitive advantage.

Key Takeaways

- Thriving under uncertainty is a proactive approach focusing on leverage, learning, and optionality rather than attempting to eliminate risk.
- A probabilistic mindset allows you to make decisions that maximize expected value while limiting downside.

- Redundant systems, iterative experimentation, and cognitive flexibility transform randomness into opportunity.
- Emotional and psychological adaptations, such as detachment from outcomes and normalization of volatility, enhance resilience and performance.

By adopting these strategies, uncertainty becomes a landscape for growth rather than a source of fear. Probabilistic resilience allows you to navigate volatility with confidence, turning unpredictability into a tool for long-term advantage and personal mastery.

16.3 Reducing Fragility in Life Systems

While anti-fragility and thriving under uncertainty focus on building strength and leveraging volatility, another crucial aspect of probabilistic resilience is **reducing fragility**. Fragility exists in any system personal, financial, social, or organizational where shocks, volatility, or unforeseen events can cause catastrophic failure. Reducing fragility is about identifying vulnerabilities, designing buffers, and creating structures that minimize downside exposure while preserving upside potential.

Identifying Fragility in Life Systems

The first step in reducing fragility is to identify weak points in your life systems. Common sources of fragility include:

- **Over-concentration:** Relying on a single income source, skill set, relationship, or market increases vulnerability to disruption.
- **Illiquidity:** Tying up resources in assets or commitments that cannot be easily adjusted or exited limits flexibility.
- **Lack of redundancy:** Absence of backup plans, alternative strategies, or support networks increases the risk of cascading failures.
- **High leverage:** Excessive debt, overcommitment, or overreliance on a single strategy amplifies negative outcomes.
- **Cognitive biases:** Overconfidence, confirmation bias, and other decision-making errors can create hidden fragilities.

By systematically examining each aspect of your life, you can uncover areas where a single shock could have disproportionate consequences.

Principles for Reducing Fragility

Once vulnerabilities are identified, the following principles can reduce fragility:

Diversification and Redundancy Spread resources, efforts, and commitments across multiple domains. Multiple income streams, diverse skills, and varied relationships create resilience. Redundancy ensures that if one path fails, others continue to function, preventing systemic collapse.

Maintain Optionality Optionality is the ability to pivot, adjust, or exit when circumstances change. It is a cornerstone of probabilistic resilience. Options may include financial flexibility, transferable skills, or modular project designs that can be scaled up or down depending on outcomes.

Build Buffers and Safety Nets Financial, physical, and social buffers absorb shocks. Emergency funds, reserves of time, supportive networks, and mental health practices create space to respond effectively to unexpected events without panic or rash decisions.

Decentralize and Distribute Risk Avoid single points of failure. In business, distribute responsibilities and decision-making; in personal life, cultivate diverse support networks and backup plans. Distributed systems are inherently less fragile.

Monitor and Adjust Continuously Fragility is dynamic. Regularly assess vulnerabilities, update plans, and learn from failures. Feedback loops allow early detection of weaknesses and enable proactive adjustments before small issues escalate into crises.

Applications in Different Life Domains

Personal Finances Avoid concentrating all wealth in a single asset or investment. Maintain a mix of liquid savings, diversified investments, and low-risk hedges. This approach limits exposure to sudden market downturns and creates optionality to seize opportunities.

Career and Skills Relying solely on one employer or skillset increases fragility. Cultivate multiple competencies, maintain professional networks, and engage in side projects that can serve as alternative paths in case of disruption.

Health and Well-being Fragile health systems arise from neglect or overreliance on temporary fixes. Balanced nutrition, regular exercise, stress management, and preventive care act as buffers, reducing the probability of catastrophic health events.

Relationships and Social Systems Dependence on a single person or small group for support creates emotional and practical fragility. Nurture broad networks and maintain diverse social connections to ensure support is available across varying circumstances.

Case Example: Fragility in Career and How to Reduce It

Imagine a mid-career professional who relies entirely on one company for income. A sudden industry downturn or corporate restructuring could lead to catastrophic loss. Applying probabilistic resilience:

- **Diversification:** Develop freelance skills, certifications, or side projects to create alternative income streams.
- **Optionality:** Network extensively to uncover opportunities outside the current role.
- **Buffers:** Maintain an emergency fund covering 6–12 months of living expenses.
- **Feedback loops:** Regularly review career risks and adjust plans based on industry trends and personal progress.

These measures transform a fragile career into a resilient, anti-fragile system capable of surviving and even thriving in uncertainty.

Key Takeaways

- Fragility exposes systems to catastrophic loss under stress; identifying vulnerabilities is the first step to resilience.
- Principles such as diversification, optionality, buffers, decentralization, and continuous monitoring reduce fragility.
- Applying these principles across finances, career, health, and social systems ensures stability while preserving upside potential.
- Probabilistic resilience is both proactive and adaptive by reducing fragility, you create a foundation to leverage uncertainty as an opportunity for growth.

Reducing fragility does not mean avoiding risk entirely; it means structuring life systems to survive shocks, learn from volatility, and retain the flexibility to seize unexpected opportunities. Combined with anti-fragility and thriving under uncertainty, this completes the framework of probabilistic resilience, empowering you to navigate a complex, unpredictable world with confidence and adaptability.

Chapter 17

Optionality & Asymmetric Bets

In an uncertain world, the most successful individuals and organizations are those who maintain the freedom to act when opportunities arise and the discipline to limit exposure to catastrophic loss. This principle is captured in the concepts of **optionality** and **asymmetric bets**. Optionality is the ability to pursue multiple pathways without committing prematurely, while asymmetric bets are investments of time, energy, or capital where potential gains far exceed potential losses.

17.1 Why Small Bets Create Large Payoffs

One of the most powerful strategies in probabilistic thinking is leveraging small, calculated bets to capture disproportionate gains. Unlike large, high-stakes commitments that can result in catastrophic loss, small bets allow for repeated experimentation, learning, and optionality, while providing the potential for exponential upside. This principle underlies the success of many entrepreneurs, investors, and innovators who consistently convert small risks into outsized rewards over time.

The Mechanics of Small Bets

Small bets work because they combine three core elements:

- **Limited downside:** The cost of the bet is small relative to your overall resources, minimizing potential harm.
- **Unlimited or large upside:** The potential gain from the bet is significantly higher than the initial investment.

- **Scalability and compounding:** Successful bets can be scaled, repeated, or leveraged to amplify returns over time.

By keeping stakes low, you gain the freedom to explore multiple opportunities without risking systemic failure. The probability of catastrophic outcomes diminishes, while the potential for unexpected windfalls grows.

Examples Across Domains

Entrepreneurship: Many successful startups begin as small bets on unproven ideas. Founders invest minimal capital to test hypotheses, validate product-market fit, or explore niche markets. If the bet succeeds, it can scale rapidly, generating disproportionate returns relative to the initial investment. If it fails, the loss is manageable and provides valuable lessons for the next attempt.

Investing: Angel investing, venture capital, and options trading are classic examples of asymmetric bets. A small stake in a high-potential startup can yield massive returns, while most other small bets may fail. The key is managing exposure so that losses remain tolerable, while wins are transformative.

Personal Development: Investing small amounts of time and energy in learning new skills, building networks, or exploring side projects can produce outsized long-term benefits. For instance, dedicating just a few hours per week to a skill that aligns with future opportunities may eventually lead to career breakthroughs or entrepreneurial ventures.

Probabilistic Logic Behind Small Bets

From a probabilistic perspective, small bets increase expected value while controlling risk. Consider a scenario:

- Each bet costs \$100, with a 10% chance of producing \$1,000.
- Expected value per bet = (0.1 × \$1,000) + (0.9 × -\$100) = \$10 - \$90 = -\$80.

At first glance, some bets may appear negative in expected value, but by carefully selecting bets where potential upside significantly outweighs downside (e.g., limited loss but large potential gain), repeated small bets compound favorable outcomes. Over time, the combination of repeated wins and scalability generates an asymmetry that cannot be achieved through single, large bets.

Psychological Advantages of Small Bets

Small bets also provide significant psychological benefits:

- **Reduced fear of failure:** When losses are manageable, decision-making remains rational rather than driven by anxiety.
- **Rapid feedback loops:** Each bet produces information, allowing quick learning and adaptation.
- **Encouragement of experimentation:** Low-cost bets incentivize exploration of novel ideas and untested approaches.

The combination of controlled risk, learning, and optionality builds a mental framework for probabilistic decision-making that compounds over time.

Case Example: The Venture Capital Model

Venture capital firms exemplify the small bet approach:

- They invest small amounts in a large portfolio of startups.
- Most startups fail, resulting in minor losses.
- A few successes generate exponential returns that outweigh the cumulative losses.

This asymmetric structure allows VC firms to thrive in a high-uncertainty environment. By scaling small bets across multiple ventures, they maximize expected value while controlling downside risk.

Key Takeaways

- Small bets are powerful because they combine limited downside with potentially unlimited upside.
- Repeated, low-cost bets allow learning, experimentation, and probabilistic optimization.
- Across entrepreneurship, investing, and personal development, small bets compound into outsized results.
- Psychological benefits include reduced fear, faster learning, and greater willingness to experiment.
- Strategically applied, small bets create a structural advantage in uncertain and volatile environments, forming the foundation of probabilistic decision-making.

In summary, small bets allow you to engage with uncertainty proactively, capturing opportunities while limiting exposure to catastrophic loss. By embedding this principle into your decision-making, you create a framework for scalable growth, compounding advantage, and long-term probabilistic success.

17.2 Preserving Flexibility in Decision-Making

In an unpredictable world, the ability to remain flexible keeping multiple options open while avoiding premature commitment is one of the most valuable skills you can develop. Flexibility in decision-making is the practical application of **optionality**: it allows you to respond to new information, capitalize on unexpected opportunities, and mitigate the impact of unforeseen risks. Without flexibility, even well-informed decisions can become liabilities when circumstances shift.

The Cost of Rigidity

Rigid decisions lock you into a single path. While commitment can sometimes be necessary, excessive rigidity introduces fragility:

- **Missed opportunities:** When circumstances change, a rigid plan can prevent you from acting on new possibilities.
- **Amplified losses:** Committing fully to a failing course of action increases downside exposure.
- **Reduced learning:** Sticking to one path limits feedback from alternative approaches, slowing probabilistic learning.

Flexibility is not indecision; it is a deliberate strategy to preserve optionality until sufficient information or clarity emerges.

Principles for Preserving Flexibility

Delay Irreversible Decisions Where possible, postpone irreversible commitments until more information is available. For example, in entrepreneurship, pilot testing a product before scaling preserves the ability to pivot. In investing, gradual allocation rather than lump-sum commitment allows adjustment to market signals.

Build Modularity Design decisions in modular components that can be adjusted independently. In a project, modular design allows individual elements to evolve without jeopardizing the entire system. In career planning, pursuing transferable skills creates flexibility across industries.

Maintain Optionality in Resources Keep financial, temporal, and mental resources available to respond to emerging opportunities. Liquid assets, time buffers, and cognitive space create the ability to act when favorable conditions arise.

Use Scenario Planning Anticipate multiple possible futures and design actions that remain effective across them. Flexibility is enhanced when decisions are robust to a range of scenarios rather than optimized for a single expected outcome.

Avoid Over-leveraging Excessive commitment of capital, time, or effort reduces adaptability. By limiting leverage, you maintain room to maneuver when conditions change, increasing your ability to exploit upside while containing downside.

Psychological Aspects of Flexibility

Flexibility requires both cognitive and emotional discipline:

- **Detachment from outcomes:** Avoid tying self-worth to a single decision or plan. This encourages rational adaptation rather than defensive rigidity.
- **Comfort with ambiguity:** Embrace uncertainty as a source of opportunity rather than a threat.
- **Iterative mindset:** Treat decisions as experiments to refine over time, rather than final judgments.

Developing these habits ensures that flexibility is applied consistently, not just sporadically under pressure.

Applications Across Domains

Investing: Instead of committing all capital to a single stock or asset class, phased investments, hedges, and diversified allocations allow adjustments as market conditions evolve.

Entrepreneurship: Startups that maintain modular products, flexible team structures, and optionality in partnerships are better positioned to pivot when markets shift, turning uncertainty into opportunity.

Career Development: Acquiring transferable skills, networking broadly, and pursuing multiple projects ensures that career trajectories remain adaptable, even in the face of industry disruption.

Personal Life Decisions: Maintaining optionality in relationships, living arrangements, or lifestyle choices enables smoother adaptation to changing circumstances, enhancing resilience and long-term satisfaction.

Case Example: Adaptive Business Strategy

Consider a tech startup launching a new software platform. By preserving flexibility:

- They release a minimum viable product (MVP) to test market response rather than committing to a full-scale rollout.
- They design features modularly, allowing adjustments based on user feedback.
- They maintain financial reserves to explore alternative features or pivot to new markets.

When early indicators show unexpected demand patterns, the company can adapt, improving the product and seizing opportunities that rigid planning would have missed.

Key Takeaways

- Flexibility is the practical manifestation of optionality; it preserves the ability to act under uncertainty.
- Rigidity increases fragility, limits learning, and amplifies losses under changing conditions.
- Principles such as delayed irreversible decisions, modular design, resource optionality, scenario planning, and limited leverage enhance adaptability.
- Cognitive and emotional discipline, including detachment from outcomes and comfort with ambiguity, are essential to sustain flexibility.
- Applied across investing, entrepreneurship, career, and personal life, flexibility allows you to convert uncertainty into a source of advantage, maximizing potential gains while containing downside risk.

In essence, preserving flexibility is about keeping doors open and options alive. It ensures that, no matter how unpredictable the environment, you remain in a position to seize opportunities, mitigate risks, and optimize outcomes over time. Flexibility is the bridge between probabilistic thinking and real-world execution, enabling optionality to translate into tangible advantage.

17.3 Positive Convexity Strategies

Positive convexity is a powerful concept in probabilistic decision-making and optionality. It refers to situations where the upside potential grows disproportionately relative to downside exposure. In other words, small changes or favorable outcomes result in outsized benefits, while unfavorable outcomes are limited or contained. Designing decisions, investments, or life systems with positive convexity allows you to leverage uncertainty, volatility, and randomness for maximum advantage.

Understanding Convexity

Convexity can be visualized geometrically: a convex function curves upward, so increases in the input produce accelerating gains in output. Applied to decision-making:

- Positive convexity: Gains accelerate with favorable events, losses are capped.
- Negative convexity: Losses accelerate with adverse events, gains are limited.

Most traditional risk-taking without optionality exhibits negative convexity: a single bad outcome can wipe out all gains. Positive convexity flips this paradigm by designing asymmetry into the system.

Principles of Positive Convexity

Limit Downside, Maximize Upside The core of convexity is asymmetric exposure. Investments, projects, or decisions should be structured so that losses are constrained while gains have the potential to scale exponentially. Examples include:

- Options contracts in finance, where the maximum loss is the premium paid but upside is potentially unlimited.
- Early-stage entrepreneurial experiments, where a small capital or time investment can generate massive returns if successful.

Optionality as a Convexity Multiplier Optionality is the mechanism that creates positive convexity. By keeping multiple pathways open, you increase the likelihood of encountering favorable outcomes that disproportionately outweigh the limited cost of the option.

Compounding Small Advantages Repeated exposure to small, positive-convexity bets compounds over time. Each successful bet builds resources, learning, and confidence, enhancing your ability to capture the next opportunity. This is the principle behind long-term probabilistic advantage.

Embrace Volatility Positive convexity thrives in environments with high volatility. Random fluctuations, market swings, or shifting conditions create asymmetric opportunities. Rather than avoiding volatility, design systems that benefit from it.

Applications Across Domains

Investing Structured products, options, and venture investments often exhibit positive convexity. By capping potential losses and retaining high-upside potential, investors convert market volatility into a source of advantage.

Entrepreneurship Launching multiple minimum viable products (MVPs) or pursuing small exploratory projects allows entrepreneurs to capitalize on outlier successes without risking total failure.

Career and Skills Investing time in high-leverage skills or networking opportunities while limiting the commitment creates scenarios where small initial efforts can result in disproportionate career advancement.

Personal Life and Health Experiments in lifestyle, such as incremental changes in fitness, nutrition, or relationships, can yield compounding positive outcomes over time while avoiding catastrophic health or social risks.

Case Example: Tech Startup Optionality

A technology startup implements positive convexity by:

- Launching multiple small features (MVPs) to test user engagement rather than committing all resources to one product.
- Structuring investments in new tools and partnerships as reversible commitments, limiting downside risk.
- Leveraging user feedback to pivot and scale the most promising features, generating outsized returns relative to the small initial investment.

This approach ensures that volatility in market demand becomes a source of opportunity rather than a threat.

Key Takeaways

- Positive convexity is the structural advantage gained when favorable outcomes produce outsized gains and unfavorable outcomes are limited.
- Optionality, small bets, and scalable experimentation are practical mechanisms to achieve convexity.
- Repeated exposure to convex opportunities compounds advantages over time, building probabilistic dominance.
- Volatility is not an enemy; when approached correctly, it amplifies positive convexity and creates asymmetric opportunities.
- Across investing, entrepreneurship, career, and personal growth, designing for positive convexity transforms uncertainty into a source of leverage and long-term success.

By integrating positive convexity strategies with small bets and preserved flexibility, you create a decision-making framework that maximizes upside, limits downside, and leverages uncertainty as a competitive advantage. These principles form the core of probabilistic mastery and optionality in life, finance, and business.

Chapter 18

Luck vs. Skill

In every domain of life finance, entrepreneurship, career progression, or personal achievements success is influenced by a combination of skill and luck. Yet, humans often misinterpret outcomes, attributing achievements entirely to skill or failures entirely to bad luck. This misperception can lead to overconfidence, poor decisions, and a fragile mindset.
Understanding the interplay between skill and luck is essential for probabilistic thinking. It allows you to distinguish between genuine competence and random outcomes, measure the repeatability of your actions, and design strategies that maximize long-term success while minimizing exposure to randomness.

18.1 Distinguishing Signal from Noise

One of the greatest challenges in probabilistic thinking is separating **signal** the meaningful information that reflects skill, causation, or predictable patterns from **noise** random fluctuations, coincidences, or misleading outcomes. Misinterpreting noise as signal can lead to overconfidence, flawed decision-making, and the illusion of control, while mistaking signal for noise may cause you to ignore real patterns and squander opportunities.

Understanding Signal and Noise

- **Signal:** The part of an outcome that is repeatable, reliable, and attributable to skill, effort, or causal factors. For example, a consistently high-performing employee demonstrates signal through predictable, skill-driven results.

- **Noise:** Random variation or luck that obscures true patterns. Noise is inherently unpredictable and may give the illusion of performance or failure. For example, a single lucky investment or unexpected market swing is noise if it does not reflect replicable skill.

Noise can be deceiving because humans are wired to see patterns even in randomness, a cognitive bias known as **apophenia**. Recognizing and filtering out noise is a fundamental skill for probabilistic decision-making.

Why Humans Confuse Noise for Signal

Several psychological tendencies contribute to misattribution:

- **Hindsight bias:** After an event, we often believe the outcome was predictable, exaggerating the role of skill.
- **Overconfidence:** Success reinforces the perception of personal competence, even when luck played a significant role.
- **Outcome bias:** We judge decisions based on results rather than the quality of the decision-making process. A good decision may fail due to bad luck, and a poor decision may succeed by chance.

Being aware of these biases is the first step toward distinguishing true signal from deceptive noise.

Techniques to Identify Signal

Analyze Long-Term Patterns Single events rarely provide reliable insight. Evaluating performance over multiple instances reduces the impact of randomness and highlights genuine skill. For example, a trader's edge is apparent only after analyzing hundreds of trades, not a single profitable day.

Compare Against Benchmarks Benchmarking against peers, historical averages, or objective metrics helps isolate skill. Deviations that consistently outperform benchmarks are more likely to reflect signal rather than luck.

Use Statistical Methods Variance, standard deviation, and regression analysis are powerful tools to quantify noise. Understanding distributions allows you to estimate which outcomes are within expected randomness and which reflect real underlying patterns.

Test Replicability A result that can be consistently replicated under varying conditions is likely skill-based. Experiments, simulations, and iterative processes help validate whether an observed outcome is genuine or random.

Focus on Process, Not Just Outcomes Evaluate the decision-making process itself. Sound methodology reduces the influence of luck and ensures that even adverse outcomes contribute to learning.

Applications Across Domains

Investing: A single winning trade may be luck; a strategy that consistently generates positive returns across different markets demonstrates skill. Proper attribution prevents overleveraging on perceived expertise.

Entrepreneurship: Startup success often involves both execution and timing. Distinguishing which factors were controllable (signal) and which were external luck (noise) allows founders to replicate success and mitigate future failures.

Career and Personal Development: Promotions or accolades may result from both talent and circumstance. Focusing on improving skills and consistently high-quality work increases the likelihood that future outcomes are skill-driven rather than random.

Key Takeaways

- Signal represents skill, causation, and repeatable patterns; noise is random variation and luck.
- Humans naturally misattribute noise as signal due to cognitive biases such as hindsight bias, overconfidence, and outcome bias.
- Long-term analysis, benchmarking, statistical evaluation, replicability testing, and process-focused assessment are essential to separate signal from noise.
- Recognizing the difference allows you to make decisions with a realistic understanding of what you control versus what is random, preventing overconfidence and improving probabilistic outcomes.

Mastering the distinction between signal and noise is the foundation for understanding luck versus skill. It allows you to act strategically, recognize when outcomes are repeatable, and allocate effort and resources where they will reliably generate returns while avoiding the traps of randomness disguised as achievement.

18.2 Measuring Repeatability

A critical aspect of distinguishing skill from luck is determining whether an outcome is **repeatable**. Repeatability measures whether a result can be consistently reproduced under similar conditions, which is the hallmark of genuine skill. Without repeatability, even extraordinary successes may be largely attributable to chance rather than expertise.

The Concept of Repeatability

Repeatability is the degree to which a process or action produces consistent results over time. It reflects the reliability of a skill, system, or strategy in generating positive outcomes. For example:

- A stock trader who earns consistent profits over hundreds of trades demonstrates repeatable skill.
- A chef who produces excellent dishes consistently, regardless of the day or kitchen conditions, shows repeatable ability.
- A startup founder who launches multiple successful ventures exhibits repeatable entrepreneurial skill.

Conversely, outcomes that are exceptional in isolation but fail to recur are more likely the result of luck.

Why Repeatability Matters

Understanding repeatability has profound implications for decision-making:

- **Resource allocation:** By focusing on repeatable strategies, you invest time, money, and energy where skill predominates, rather than chasing one-off lucky events.
- **Risk management:** Repeatable processes reduce exposure to downside randomness because outcomes are predictable within a probabilistic range.
- **Learning and improvement:** Measuring repeatable results allows iterative refinement. Inconsistent outcomes are harder to analyze, making skill development more difficult.

Without assessing repeatability, you risk attributing success to skill when it is actually noise, or dismissing a genuine process as luck.

Techniques to Measure Repeatability

Track Longitudinal Performance Observe results over time rather than relying on single outcomes. Longitudinal tracking reduces the influence of random variation and provides a clearer picture of skill consistency.

Use Statistical Analysis Variance, standard deviation, and confidence intervals help quantify consistency. High repeatability is indicated by low variance in outcomes relative to expected performance.

Establish Benchmarks and Controls Comparing performance against industry standards, peer groups, or historical data helps isolate skill from environmental luck. Controls reduce the influence of extraneous factors.

Test Across Contexts Skill is more likely genuine if it transfers across situations, markets, or conditions. For instance, an investor who consistently succeeds in multiple market cycles demonstrates repeatable expertise.

Evaluate Process Rigor Focus on whether a well-defined process produces consistent outcomes. A strong process ensures that results are less dependent on random externalities, enhancing repeatability.

Applications Across Domains

Investing: An investor should measure the repeatability of their strategy across different assets, timeframes, and market conditions. A single winning trade is meaningless without a pattern of consistent performance.

Entrepreneurship: Entrepreneurs should analyze whether their success derives from replicable business practices market research, product development processes, customer acquisition strategies or from favorable timing and chance.

Sports and Skills Development: Athletes or professionals measure repeatability through consistent performance metrics speed, accuracy, or output quality rather than occasional extraordinary feats.

Personal Life Decisions: Repeated habits and routines exercise, learning, or financial discipline produce predictable outcomes. One-off successes or failures may mislead, but repeatable behaviors compound into long-term advantage.

Key Takeaways

- Repeatability is the defining measure of whether outcomes are skill-driven rather than luck-driven.
- Tracking long-term performance, applying statistical analysis, benchmarking, testing across contexts, and evaluating processes help quantify repeatability.
- Focusing on repeatable strategies allows better allocation of resources, risk management, and skill development.
- Understanding repeatability reduces overconfidence and increases probabilistic discipline, allowing more rational decision-making in uncertain environments.
- Repeatable actions are the building blocks of compounding advantage, forming a foundation for sustainable success in investing, entrepreneurship, careers, and personal growth.

In essence, measuring repeatability separates those who consistently create value from those who succeed merely by chance. It allows you to identify genuine skill, allocate effort effectively, and design strategies that reliably capture opportunity while respecting the role of randomness.

18.3 Learning to Respect Randomness

Randomness is an unavoidable aspect of life, finance, business, and personal endeavors. Even the most skilled individuals operate in environments influenced by uncertainty, chance events, and factors beyond their control. Learning to respect randomness is not about becoming passive or fatalistic; rather, it is about cultivating humility, discipline, and probabilistic thinking to make decisions that account for the unpredictable.

Why Respecting Randomness Matters

Failing to acknowledge randomness can lead to critical errors:

- **Overconfidence:** Attributing all successes to skill inflates ego and encourages reckless decision-making.
- **Misguided replication:** Attempting to replicate outcomes driven by luck wastes resources and time.
- **Underestimation of risk:** Ignoring randomness can expose you to extreme downside events, particularly when negative outcomes are rare but severe.

Respecting randomness allows you to distinguish controllable factors from uncontrollable ones, focus on skillful actions, and design systems that are resilient to uncertainty.

Principles for Respecting Randomness

Embrace Probabilistic Thinking View outcomes as distributions rather than certainties. Every decision carries a range of possible results. Probabilistic thinking forces you to consider both the likelihood and magnitude of potential outcomes, reducing reliance on intuition alone.

Focus on Process over Outcome Evaluate decisions based on the quality of the process rather than the immediate result. A well-designed decision process produces favorable long-term results, even if individual outcomes fluctuate due to randomness.

Prepare for Extremes Randomness often manifests in extreme events, or "tail events." Respecting randomness involves planning for worst-case scenarios while positioning yourself to benefit from favorable outliers, thereby creating asymmetric opportunities.

Cultivate Humility and Patience Accept that outcomes are influenced by luck. Avoid overreacting to short-term successes or failures. Maintain a long-term perspective, understanding that repeated exposure to well-structured processes will favor skill over time.

Learn from Data, Not Anecdotes Individual stories can mislead. Focus on aggregated results, longitudinal studies, and statistically significant patterns to identify genuine skill and reduce the influence of noise.

Applications Across Domains

Investing: Even experienced investors cannot predict markets with certainty. By respecting randomness, they diversify portfolios, manage risk, and avoid overleveraging based on short-term performance.

Entrepreneurship: Startups succeed and fail due to a combination of execution and external factors. Entrepreneurs who respect randomness design experiments, maintain optionality, and iterate based on evidence rather than luck-driven outcomes.

Career Development: Promotions, opportunities, and successes often involve timing and circumstance. Focusing on skill development, networking, and adaptable strategies allows you to benefit from chance events without being controlled by them.

Personal Life and Health: Random life events accidents, illnesses, or sudden opportunities are inevitable. Planning for contingencies, maintaining healthy habits, and investing in resilient systems allows you to manage risk and capitalize on favorable circumstances.

Key Takeaways

- Randomness is omnipresent and impacts all decisions, even when skill is involved.
- Respecting randomness prevents overconfidence, misattribution, and catastrophic exposure.
- Probabilistic thinking, process-focused evaluation, preparation for extremes, humility, patience, and data-driven analysis are essential tools for managing randomness.
- Incorporating randomness into strategy allows you to reduce downside risk while positioning yourself to benefit from favorable outliers.
- Over time, those who respect randomness and design for it consistently outperform those who ignore or underestimate its role.

In essence, respecting randomness transforms uncertainty from a source of fear into a tool for advantage. It instills discipline, enhances probabilistic judgment, and ensures that luck works for you rather than against you. By combining this respect with the principles of skill assessment and repeatability, you can navigate complex environments with confidence and resilience.

Chapter 19

Compounding Mental Edge

In finance, we understand the power of compounding: small gains, consistently reinvested over time, can grow into enormous wealth. Similarly, in the realm of thought, decision-making, and personal effectiveness, mental habits, frameworks, and probabilistic thinking can compound, creating a **mental edge** that grows exponentially over a lifetime.

The concept of a compounding mental edge revolves around the deliberate accumulation of small, consistent advantages in how you think, decide, and learn. Just as small differences in returns can drastically change financial outcomes, minor improvements in probabilistic reasoning, cognitive frameworks, and disciplined decision-making multiply over time, providing outsized long-term benefits.

19.1 Mental Models as Compounding Assets

Mental models are frameworks or lenses through which we interpret the world, make decisions, and solve problems. They are the building blocks of rational thought, enabling us to simplify complexity, predict outcomes, and take probabilistic action. Over time, these models do not merely assist decision-making they compound, becoming a durable **mental edge** that grows exponentially with experience, reflection, and application.

The Concept of Mental Models

A mental model is a simplified representation of reality that helps us understand, analyze, and respond effectively to situations. Examples include:

- **Opportunity cost:** Understanding that every choice has a trade-off.

- **Second-order thinking:** Anticipating the consequences of consequences.
- **Probabilistic thinking:** Evaluating outcomes in terms of likelihood and impact rather than certainty.
- **Optionality:** Valuing flexibility and asymmetric opportunities.

Each model is a lens that filters information and guides decision-making. Individually, one model offers limited advantage, but collectively, they compound by improving decisions, reducing errors, and enhancing learning across diverse domains.

How Mental Models Compound

The compounding effect arises from three mechanisms:

Repeated Application Every decision or problem tackled using a mental model reinforces the cognitive pathway, making it faster and more accurate over time. Just as compound interest grows on principal, small, consistent applications of mental models generate incremental gains that accumulate into significant advantages.

Cross-Domain Leverage Mental models are often transferable across domains. A framework learned in investing such as risk-reward asymmetry can be applied to entrepreneurship, career decisions, or personal life choices. This cross-domain compounding accelerates cognitive growth far beyond single-context expertise.

Reducing Cognitive Errors Each mental model acts as a check against biases, fallacies, and flawed reasoning. By systematically applying multiple models, you reduce costly mistakes, enhancing long-term decision quality. Avoiding errors compounds advantage similarly to consistent small gains in finance.

Examples of Mental Models as Compounding Assets

Investing: An investor who consistently applies models like expected value, convexity, and optionality builds a portfolio not just of assets, but of cognitive leverage. Over decades, even small edges compound into substantial financial outperformance.

Entrepreneurship: Entrepreneurs using models like minimum viable bets (MVBs), feedback loops, and tail risk awareness make better strategic choices. Each successful decision reinforces learning, improving the probability of future success.

Personal Life: Cognitive models in habit formation, risk management, and probabilistic reasoning help individuals navigate uncertainty in health, relationships, and career. Over years, these small advantages accumulate, producing outsized life outcomes.

Key Takeaways

- Mental models are cognitive tools that simplify reality and improve decision-making.
- Repeated application, cross-domain leverage, and error reduction allow mental models to compound over time.
- A diverse collection of mental models forms a durable competitive edge, enhancing probabilistic thinking and long-term outcomes.
- Investing in your cognitive toolkit is analogous to investing in financial assets small, consistent efforts yield exponential returns over time.
- Compounding mental advantage allows you to act with clarity, discipline, and foresight, even in uncertain and high-variance environments.

By treating mental models as compounding assets, you transform your mind into a system capable of generating repeated, probabilistic advantages. This approach turns learning, reflection, and deliberate practice into a long-term strategy for success across business, investing, and life.

19.2 Small Probability Advantages Over Time

Success in complex systems rarely results from single, large wins. Instead, it is the accumulation of many small edges tiny advantages that, when repeated consistently, compound into substantial long-term outcomes. Understanding and leveraging **small probability advantages** is a cornerstone of probabilistic thinking and a powerful driver of compounding mental and material wealth.

The Concept of Small Edges

A small probability advantage is a marginal improvement in decision-making, execution, or outcome likelihood that slightly tilts the odds in your favor. Alone, it may seem negligible, but when applied consistently over time, these small advantages multiply exponentially.

- In investing, a 1% edge in expected value per trade may seem trivial, but over hundreds of trades, it can lead to significant cumulative gains.

- In entrepreneurship, slightly better customer acquisition strategies or operational efficiencies compound over multiple product launches.
- In personal development, incremental improvements in learning, habits, and productivity accumulate into transformative life outcomes.

The principle mirrors financial compounding: small incremental gains, consistently applied, grow far faster than one-off large gains.

Why Small Edges Matter More Than Big Wins

Relying on rare, high-impact events lottery-style wins creates fragile strategies. Conversely, small advantages compound resilience, skill, and predictable growth.

- **Stability:** Small edges reduce dependency on luck or outliers, creating robust, sustainable progress.
- **Scalability:** Repeated small improvements are easier to replicate across domains or time horizons.
- **Feedback and learning:** Small, iterative advantages provide continuous feedback, allowing refinement and adaptation.

In probabilistic thinking, prioritizing marginal improvements is often more effective than chasing rare, dramatic successes. Small edges stack, while rare wins are unreliable and non-repeatable.

Techniques for Creating Small Probability Advantages

Focus on Process Optimization Refine processes incrementally. Small improvements in workflow, analysis, or decision-making increase efficiency and reduce error. Over time, these gains become significant.

Apply Mental Models Consistently Using mental models like optionality, second-order thinking, and inversion repeatedly creates a systematic edge. Each application may yield minor improvements, but cumulatively, they produce outsized advantages.

Quantify Probabilistic Outcomes Identify situations where slight adjustments can improve expected value. For example, adjusting risk-reward ratios in investing or negotiating slightly better contract terms repeatedly produces measurable advantages.

Leverage Iterative Learning Adopt a feedback-driven approach. Each iteration, experiment, or decision becomes an opportunity to incrementally improve outcomes, gradually stacking small advantages.

Embrace Redundancy and Optionality Create multiple small bets or options. Each one may carry a slight edge, but collectively, they increase the probability of favorable outcomes and reduce dependency on singular successes.

Applications Across Domains

Investing: Investors who consistently apply probabilistic reasoning and marginal improvements slightly better diversification, timing, or allocation compound small edges into long-term outperformance.

Entrepreneurship: Startups that optimize processes, iterate products, and make slightly better strategic decisions repeatedly accumulate a competitive advantage that competitors cannot easily match.

Career and Personal Development: Small, consistent improvements in skill, knowledge, and habits reading, networking, or learning compound into significant professional and personal growth over years.

Decision-Making in Complex Systems: Even a small advantage in probabilistic reasoning can prevent large errors, mitigate tail risks, and exploit favorable outliers. Over time, these small edges create disproportionate long-term rewards.

Key Takeaways

- Small probability advantages are marginal improvements that tilt the odds in your favor.
- Consistently applying these edges compounds them over time, creating exponential growth in skill, wealth, and decision quality.
- Focusing on incremental improvements reduces reliance on luck and creates robust, repeatable systems for success.
- Iterative learning, process optimization, probabilistic reasoning, and optionality are practical ways to generate small edges.
- Over the long term, compounding small advantages often outperforms attempts to achieve rare, large wins, providing both resilience and superior outcomes.

By mastering the art of accumulating small edges, you develop a compounding mental advantage. This principle transforms incremental, probabilistic improvements into long-term exponential outcomes mirroring the power of compounding in finance, but applied to the mind itself.

19.3 Cognitive Compounding vs. Financial Compounding

Most people understand the power of financial compounding: investing a small sum, earning a modest return, and reinvesting gains repeatedly results in exponential growth over time. Cognitive compounding follows a similar principle, but instead of capital, it involves **knowledge, mental models, habits, and probabilistic reasoning**. Just as money grows when invested wisely, the mind grows when ideas, skills, and insights are consistently applied and reinvested into future decisions.

The Mechanics of Cognitive Compounding

Cognitive compounding occurs when small, repeated improvements in thinking or knowledge accumulate to create outsized long-term advantages. This process works through several mechanisms:

Incremental Knowledge Accumulation Learning new concepts, frameworks, and skills gradually increases mental capacity. Each new mental model allows better interpretation of reality, improving decision-making and problem-solving capabilities. Over time, even small insights accumulate into a deep, interconnected cognitive toolkit.

Improved Decision Quality Repeated application of mental models and probabilistic thinking refines judgment. Each decision, informed by accumulated knowledge, produces better outcomes than the previous one. Even if individual results fluctuate due to randomness, the long-term trajectory improves consistently.

Feedback Loops and Iteration Cognitive compounding is accelerated by feedback. By reflecting on outcomes, analyzing mistakes, and iteratively refining mental models, each decision reinforces future capability. This recursive improvement multiplies the value of prior learning, similar to reinvesting financial returns.

Cross-Domain Leverage Cognitive gains are transferable across domains. A mental model learned in investing may enhance entrepreneurial strategy; probabilistic reasoning in risk management may improve personal decisions. Cross-domain application amplifies the compounding effect, creating leverage far beyond the initial context.

Financial Compounding	Cognitive Compounding
Invested capital grows via interest or returns	Invested time, attention, and thought grow via skill and insight
Exponential growth over long horizons	Exponential improvement in decision-making and problem-solving
Gains depend on rate of return and time	Gains depend on quality of mental models, feedback, and application
Risk exists if capital is misallocated	Risk exists if cognitive effort is misdirected or unstructured
Passive compounding possible (e.g., interest)	Active engagement required; compounding accelerates with deliberate practice

Table 19.1: Comparison of Financial and Cognitive Compounding

Financial vs. Cognitive Compounding: Parallels and Contrasts

While the mechanisms differ money grows automatically when invested correctly, whereas the mind requires active cultivation the underlying principle is identical: small, repeated advantages multiply over time to produce outsized outcomes.

Maximizing Cognitive Compounding

Invest Consistently in Learning Read broadly, study mental models, and engage in deliberate practice. Even incremental knowledge gains compound over years into a substantial cognitive edge.

Apply Knowledge Actively Theory alone does not compound. Apply insights to decisions, problems, and experiments. Each application reinforces understanding and builds experience.

Reflect and Iterate Analyze outcomes, refine strategies, and improve mental models. Iterative reflection accelerates compounding by converting mistakes into future advantages.

Diversify Cognitive Investments Just as financial portfolios benefit from diversification, diversify your mental toolkit. Learn frameworks across multiple domains to maximize transferability and adaptability.

Focus on Probabilistic Thinking Edge-based, probabilistic approaches enhance compounding by increasing the likelihood of favorable outcomes while minimizing downside risks, creating asymmetric growth in cognitive capability.

Applications Across Life Domains

Investing: Investors who continually refine mental models and probabilistic frameworks develop a compounding cognitive advantage that allows them to outperform markets consistently.

Entrepreneurship: Entrepreneurs who learn from successes and failures, iteratively improve strategies, and apply lessons across ventures create an exponential cognitive return on experience.

Personal Life: Habit formation, decision-making under uncertainty, and learning new skills all compound. Over decades, small, consistent cognitive improvements create outsized life advantages.

Key Takeaways

- Cognitive compounding mirrors financial compounding: small, repeated improvements produce exponential long-term growth.
- Knowledge, mental models, and probabilistic reasoning are the principal assets that compound.
- Cross-domain application, iterative learning, and active application maximize the compounding effect.
- Unlike money, the mind requires deliberate investment, reflection, and experimentation.
- Over time, cognitive compounding provides a sustainable competitive edge, magnifying decision quality, resilience, and long-term success.

By treating your mind as a compounding asset and consistently applying probabilistic reasoning, mental models, and reflective practice, you create exponential advantages. Cognitive compounding transforms learning and experience into enduring capability ultimately becoming the most powerful form of long-term wealth.

Chapter 20

Living with Uncertainty

Uncertainty is the only certainty in life. Every decision, every relationship, and every opportunity carries unknown outcomes. Most people resist this reality, seeking comfort in predictability, control, and certainty. But true mastery lies in embracing uncertainty not as a source of fear, but as a source of freedom, growth, and strategic advantage.

20.1 Embracing Uncertainty as Liberation

Uncertainty is often perceived as a threat a force that disrupts plans, creates anxiety, and fosters fear. Most people spend their lives attempting to control, predict, or eliminate it. Yet, this resistance is not only futile but also limiting. Paradoxically, embracing uncertainty can be one of the most liberating decisions you make. When you accept that the future is inherently unpredictable, you free yourself from the illusion of control and open the door to opportunity, creativity, and growth.

The Paradox of Control

Human nature drives us to seek certainty. We make detailed plans, seek guarantees, and attempt to forecast outcomes. While some level of planning is valuable, excessive fixation on control breeds rigidity and fear of failure. Uncertainty, when resisted, becomes a source of stress rather than a natural part of life's complexity.

Liberation comes when you shift focus from trying to control outcomes to mastering the decisions and actions within your control. By detaching from the illusion that the future is predictable, you gain mental freedom the ability to act decisively, experiment boldly, and adapt swiftly without being paralyzed by the unknown.

Opportunity Hidden in Uncertainty

Uncertainty is not merely a challenge; it is a fertile ground for opportunity. Consider:

- **Entrepreneurs:** High-variance environments like startups are filled with uncertainty. Those who embrace it can test ideas, iterate, and pivot, discovering opportunities invisible to risk-averse competitors.
- **Investors:** Probabilistic thinking allows them to identify asymmetric bets where small investments in uncertain outcomes have outsized potential payoffs.
- **Personal life:** Embracing uncertainty in career or relationship decisions encourages exploration, learning, and growth, rather than being confined to "safe" but limiting choices.

In all cases, uncertainty becomes an ally rather than an obstacle when approached with a mindset that values process over guaranteed results.

Shifting Mindsets: From Fear to Freedom

Embracing uncertainty requires a deliberate shift in mindset:

1. **Accept probabilistic outcomes:** Recognize that most decisions have multiple possible results. Focus on improving the likelihood of favorable outcomes, rather than obsessing over certainty.
2. **Prioritize optionality:** Maintain flexibility to adapt and pivot as new information emerges. Optionality is a strategic hedge against unpredictable events.
3. **Value learning over immediate results:** See failures and unexpected outcomes as feedback, not final verdicts. Learning compounds over time, building long-term advantage.
4. **Detach from ego and outcomes:** True liberation comes from focusing on quality decision-making and execution rather than attachment to a specific outcome.

The Freedom of Probabilistic Living

When you embrace uncertainty, life transforms from a rigid, high-stress path to a dynamic landscape of possibilities. Every decision becomes an experiment, every setback a lesson, and every opportunity a chance to compound small edges. Freedom is found not in controlling the world, but in mastering your response to its unpredictability.

By accepting uncertainty as an intrinsic part of life, you liberate yourself from fear, cultivate resilience, and gain the clarity to make better, probabilistic decisions. This mindset allows you to act boldly, adapt fluidly, and thrive in a world where nothing is guaranteed.

20.2 Freedom in Probabilistic Living

Probabilistic living is the art of making decisions and taking action with a clear understanding of uncertainty and risk. It is not about eliminating randomness or predicting the future with certainty; rather, it is about embracing the likelihood of multiple outcomes and positioning yourself to benefit from favorable possibilities while mitigating downside risks. Paradoxically, understanding uncertainty and probability brings freedom freedom from fear, paralysis, and the illusion of control.

The Paradox of Freedom

Most people equate freedom with certainty. They think that having a predictable job, a guaranteed income, or a fixed plan will create security and autonomy. In reality, this kind of certainty is often fragile. A sudden change in circumstances a market crash, a health issue, or an unexpected life event can shatter carefully constructed plans.
Probabilistic living shifts the definition of freedom from controlling outcomes to controlling decisions and processes. By acknowledging the probabilistic nature of life, you gain the ability to make choices that are robust across a range of scenarios, rather than being tied to one "ideal" outcome. This mindset liberates you from fear of the unknown, enabling action even in complex or high-variance situations.

Principles of Probabilistic Freedom

1. **Focus on decisions, not outcomes:** You cannot control randomness, but you can control the quality of your decisions. Evaluating choices based on expected value and edge maximization gives you freedom from obsessing over unpredictable results.

2. **Embrace optionality:** Maintain flexibility to pivot, adapt, or switch strategies. Optionality allows you to capture upside while limiting downside, creating a form of freedom rooted in adaptability.

3. **Develop mental resilience:** Probabilistic living requires detachment from immediate outcomes. By focusing on process and learning, you reduce the emotional volatility that comes from relying on singular results.

4. **Iterate and experiment:** Treat life decisions as experiments with measurable outcomes. Even failures yield data that can improve future choices, freeing you from the fear of making mistakes.

5. **Leverage compounding advantages:** Small, repeated probabilistic edges whether in investing, career, or personal growth compound over time, creating cumulative freedom and opportunity that cannot be achieved through rigid planning.

Applications in Daily Life

Career: Rather than striving for the "perfect job," probabilistic living encourages building skills, networks, and optionality. By diversifying experiences and keeping multiple paths open, you gain freedom to pivot when opportunities or risks arise.

Investing and Finance: Instead of seeking certainty in markets, investors embrace risk management, asymmetric bets, and probabilistic reasoning. This allows them to exploit opportunities without being paralyzed by volatility.

Relationships and Personal Life: Probabilistic thinking encourages exploration, experimentation, and open-mindedness. Recognizing that outcomes in relationships and social interactions are uncertain allows you to act boldly while mitigating emotional or social downside.

The Psychological Benefits of Probabilistic Freedom

Living probabilistically reduces anxiety, stress, and overthinking. When you accept that outcomes are inherently uncertain:

- You stop over-investing mentally in uncontrollable events.
- You develop resilience against setbacks and volatility.
- You cultivate curiosity and exploration, seeing uncertainty as an opportunity rather than a threat.
- You build confidence to take calculated risks without being paralyzed by fear of failure.

In essence, freedom in probabilistic living is the freedom to act decisively, adapt continuously, and thrive despite unpredictability. By shifting focus from rigid plans to flexible strategies, you create a life that is both resilient and opportunistic one where uncertainty is no longer a source of fear but a source of power.

Embracing this mindset transforms uncertainty from an obstacle into a tool for personal and professional growth. Each decision, each experiment, and each calculated risk becomes a step toward a freer, more empowered life.

20.3 Building a Philosophy of Resilience

Resilience is the ability to withstand shocks, recover from setbacks, and continue moving forward in the face of uncertainty. It is not merely endurance; it is the proactive capacity to adapt, learn, and even thrive under volatility. In a world where unpredictability is the norm, building a personal philosophy of resilience is essential for living confidently and effectively.

Resilience as a Mindset

At its core, resilience begins with perception. Those who see uncertainty as a threat become anxious and reactive, while those who see it as an opportunity become adaptive and strategic. A resilient mindset:

- Accepts that setbacks and failures are inevitable.
- Views obstacles as feedback rather than punishment.
- Focuses on controllable actions rather than uncontrollable outcomes.
- Maintains composure under stress and complexity.

By cultivating this mindset, you convert unpredictability from a source of fear into a driver of growth.

Principles of a Resilient Philosophy

1. **Anticipate variability:** Expect that life is uncertain. Mentally rehearse possible scenarios and prepare flexible strategies.
2. **Build redundancies and optionality:** Just as resilient systems have backups and buffers, individuals benefit from multiple pathways to success. Diversify skills, relationships, and resources.
3. **Focus on process over outcomes:** Evaluate decisions based on quality and rigor, not just results. Outcomes are influenced by chance; processes are within your control.
4. **Learn continuously:** Treat failures and surprises as data. Iterative learning compounds cognitive resilience over time.
5. **Manage emotions:** Detachment and emotional regulation prevent reactive decisions. Resilience grows when you respond thoughtfully rather than impulsively.

Resilience in Action

Career and Entrepreneurship: Resilient individuals and organizations survive volatility by testing assumptions, iterating quickly, and pivoting when necessary. They see setbacks not as endpoints but as information-rich events that guide future decisions.

Investing and Finance: Investors with a resilience-focused mindset accept that losses are part of probabilistic outcomes. They design portfolios to survive downturns, hedge risks, and capitalize on asymmetric opportunities over time.

Personal Life and Health: Resilience extends beyond work and wealth. Physical and mental well-being, social relationships, and personal growth all benefit from systems that anticipate stress, allow recovery, and promote adaptability.

The Role of Philosophy in Resilience

Building resilience is not just about tactics it is about cultivating an overarching philosophy:

- **Embrace uncertainty:** Accept unpredictability as inherent, not exceptional.
- **Detach from ego:** Focus on learning and improvement rather than validation or reputation.
- **Value long-term compounding:** Small, consistent advantages in decisions, habits, and mental models accumulate to create lasting resilience.
- **Integrate reflection and foresight:** Use past experiences to anticipate future variability and adapt strategies accordingly.

Key Takeaways

- Resilience is both a mindset and a system mental, emotional, and operational.
- It transforms uncertainty from a source of anxiety into a platform for growth and opportunity.
- Principles of resilience include anticipating variability, building optionality, focusing on process, learning continuously, and managing emotions.

- A resilient philosophy emphasizes long-term compounding of knowledge, skills, and probabilistic advantages.
- By embedding resilience into every aspect of life, you cultivate the ability not just to survive uncertainty, but to thrive within it.

Ultimately, building a philosophy of resilience is about aligning your mindset, systems, and actions with the reality of an unpredictable world. It empowers you to navigate complexity with confidence, adapt to change gracefully, and transform challenges into stepping stones for long-term growth and fulfillment.

Conclusion

20.4 The Journey Toward Probabilistic Thinking

Adopting a probabilistic mindset is not an event it is a lifelong journey. It requires a fundamental shift in how you perceive the world, evaluate decisions, and respond to uncertainty. Throughout this book, we have explored the principles, mental models, and strategies that allow you to navigate life with clarity, resilience, and strategic insight.

The journey begins with awareness. Recognizing the limitations of deterministic thinking and the illusion of certainty is the first step toward freedom. Once you accept that randomness, risk, and volatility are inherent in every decision, you can begin to reason probabilistically, focusing on expected value, optionality, and asymmetry rather than absolute guarantees.

Key milestones on this journey include:

- **Foundational Understanding:** Appreciating chaos, randomness, and complexity in natural and human systems.
- **Cognitive Discipline:** Overcoming biases, embracing mental models, and thinking in distributions rather than fixed points.
- **Applied Probabilistic Thinking:** Leveraging probabilistic reasoning in personal life, investing, entrepreneurship, and negotiation.
- **Resilience and Optionality:** Building systems, habits, and strategies that thrive under uncertainty and capitalize on small, repeated advantages.
- **Cognitive Compounding:** Recognizing that the consistent application of probabilistic thinking compounds over time, enhancing decision quality and long-term success.

The journey is iterative. Each decision, each setback, and each unexpected outcome is an opportunity to learn, refine your models, and improve your probabilistic reasoning. Over time, small edges accumulate, producing outsized advantages in life, work, and personal fulfillment.

20.5 Living With Confidence in an Uncertain World

Embracing a probabilistic mindset ultimately allows you to live with confidence not because the world is predictable, but because you are equipped to navigate it intelligently. Confidence in uncertainty arises from process mastery rather than outcome obsession, from preparation rather than control, and from flexibility rather than rigidity.
A confident probabilistic thinker:

- Makes decisions grounded in expected value and probabilistic reasoning.
- Accepts failure and randomness as integral to learning and growth.
- Maintains emotional equilibrium, detaching self-worth from immediate outcomes.
- Exploits opportunities that emerge from volatility while mitigating downside risks.
- Continuously refines mental models, habits, and decision frameworks to compound cognitive advantage.

Living confidently in an uncertain world does not mean avoiding risks or expecting success in every endeavor. It means understanding the probabilistic nature of reality, taking calculated actions, and cultivating resilience so that you can thrive despite the inherent unpredictability of life.
In essence, probabilistic thinking is more than a set of tools or techniques it is a philosophy of life. It transforms fear into freedom, randomness into opportunity, and small, repeated advantages into long-term success. By internalizing this mindset, you equip yourself to navigate complexity, seize asymmetric opportunities, and live a life of purpose, clarity, and confidence even when the future is unknown.

Final Thought: The journey toward probabilistic thinking is ongoing. Each day presents new uncertainties, new decisions, and new opportunities to apply what you have learned. Approach them with curiosity, discipline, and courage. Over time, your probabilistic mindset will not only guide your decisions but also shape the trajectory of your life, allowing you to thrive in a world where nothing is certain but everything is possible.

Key Takeaways

The probabilistic mindset is not just a way of thinking it is a practical approach to decision-making, risk management, and life strategy. This appendix distills the essential lessons from the book into actionable takeaways that can be applied immediately in personal, professional, and financial contexts.

Embrace Uncertainty as a Feature, Not a Flaw

- Accept that randomness, risk, and unpredictability are inherent in every decision.
- Focus on actions within your control rather than obsessing over outcomes.
- Treat unexpected events as opportunities for learning and adaptation.

Think in Probabilities, Not Absolutes

- Avoid deterministic thinking; understand that most outcomes are probabilistic.
- Use expected value to guide decisions rather than relying solely on intuition or anecdotal evidence.
- Consider ranges, distributions, and variance when assessing possibilities.

Apply Mental Models Consistently

- Use inversion, second-order thinking, and other probabilistic mental models to evaluate decisions from multiple angles.
- Develop cognitive frameworks that help distinguish signal from noise.

- Combine multiple mental models for layered insights and robust decision-making.

Manage Cognitive Biases and Emotional Traps

- Be aware of overconfidence, hindsight bias, loss aversion, and probability neglect.
- Separate outcomes from processes to reduce emotional attachment to specific results.
- Regularly check assumptions and challenge intuitions with data and probabilistic reasoning.

Build Optionality and Exploit Asymmetry

- Take small, calculated bets that offer large upside potential (asymmetric opportunities).
- Maintain flexibility to pivot, adapt, and capitalize on unforeseen events.
- Design life, career, and financial systems with optionality to minimize fragility.

Compounding Small Advantages

- Consistently apply small probabilistic edges; their impact compounds over time.
- Learn iteratively from outcomes, refining decision frameworks with each cycle.
- Recognize that cognitive compounding through better models, habits, and skills can exceed the power of financial compounding.

Integrate Probabilistic Thinking Across Life Domains

- **Career:** Treat your career as a portfolio of options and bets rather than a single linear path.
- **Investing:** Focus on expected value, risk-adjusted returns, and portfolio resilience.
- **Entrepreneurship:** Experiment with high-variance projects and leverage minimum viable bets.

- **Relationships and Health:** Apply risk-reward thinking to personal choices and social connections, balancing long-term benefits and short-term variability.

Cultivate Resilience and Freedom

- Develop systems and habits that survive volatility and uncertainty.
- Build emotional detachment from outcomes while committing fully to decision quality.
- View setbacks as feedback and opportunities for growth rather than failures.

Live Confidently in an Uncertain World

- Recognize that certainty is an illusion and freedom comes from understanding probabilities.
- Make decisions decisively, iterate continuously, and embrace the lessons of randomness.
- Treat probabilistic thinking as a lifelong practice that compounds mental, financial, and personal advantages over time.

Final Note: The probabilistic mindset transforms fear into opportunity, complexity into clarity, and small decisions into compounding advantage. By internalizing these key takeaways and applying them consistently, you equip yourself to navigate an unpredictable world with confidence, resilience, and strategic insight.

Recommended Readings & Resources

The probabilistic mindset is a lifelong practice. While this book provides a blueprint for thinking, decision-making, and living under uncertainty, there is immense value in exploring other works, research, and tools that deepen your understanding. The following recommended readings and resources cover probability, decision theory, risk management, behavioral economics, mental models, entrepreneurship, and cognitive frameworks.

Books on Probability, Risk, and Decision-Making

- **"Fooled by Randomness" by Nassim Nicholas Taleb** – Explores the role of luck and randomness in markets and life, emphasizing how humans misinterpret probability and success.
- **"The Black Swan" by Nassim Nicholas Taleb** – A deeper dive into rare, high-impact events and their outsized influence on history, finance, and personal decisions.
- **"Thinking, Fast and Slow" by Daniel Kahneman** – Investigates cognitive biases, heuristics, and the psychology of judgment under uncertainty.
- **"Superforecasting" by Philip E. Tetlock and Dan Gardner** – Shows how probabilistic thinking and disciplined forecasting improve decision-making accuracy.
- **"Risk Savvy" by Gerd Gigerenzer** – Offers practical strategies to navigate risk, probability, and statistics in everyday life.

Books on Mental Models and Strategic Thinking

- **"Poor Charlie's Almanack" by Charlie Munger** – A treasure trove of mental models, multidisciplinary thinking, and probabilistic reasoning applied to investing and life.
- **"Seeking Wisdom" by Peter Bevelin** – Explores mental models, cognitive biases, and decision-making frameworks to improve thinking quality.
- **"The Great Mental Models" series by Shane Parrish** – Practical guides for applying mental models to problem-solving, decision-making, and strategy.

Books on Entrepreneurship and Innovation

- **"The Lean Startup" by Eric Ries** – Introduces iterative testing, minimum viable products, and learning-driven strategies for startups.
- **"Antifragile" by Nassim Nicholas Taleb** – Explains how systems and organizations can thrive under volatility and uncertainty.
- **"Zero to One" by Peter Thiel** – Offers insights on creating high-value, asymmetric opportunities through innovation.

Online Resources and Tools

- **Farnam Street (www.farnamstreetblog.com)** – A resource for mental models, decision-making frameworks, and strategic thinking.
- **Khan Academy: Probability & Statistics** – Free tutorials to build foundational knowledge in probability and statistical reasoning.
- **Coursera and edX Courses on Decision Science and Risk Management** – Platforms offering courses on probability, risk, and data-driven decision-making.
- **Financial Modeling and Simulation Tools** – Tools such as Monte Carlo simulators, Excel add-ins, and Python libraries for modeling uncertainty and expected value.

Journals and Research Papers

- **Journal of Behavioral Decision Making** – Academic research on decision-making under uncertainty.
- **Management Science and Strategic Management Journals** – Studies on organizational strategy, risk, and probabilistic approaches.
- **NBER Working Papers** – Research on finance, risk, and asymmetric decision-making.

Final Note: The journey toward probabilistic thinking is continuous. Engaging with these books, courses, and tools will expand your mental models, deepen your understanding of risk and uncertainty, and strengthen your ability to make high-quality decisions in complex, unpredictable environments. Make exploration and learning a habit your probabilistic edge grows as your knowledge compounds over time.

Notes

This section provides references, citations, and explanatory notes for the concepts, examples, and research discussed throughout *The Probabilistic Mind.* Notes are organized by chapter and section to allow readers to explore sources in more depth.

Introduction and Foundations

1. Taleb, Nassim Nicholas. *Fooled by Randomness.* New York: Random House, 2001. – Discusses the pervasive role of randomness in financial markets and life.

2. Kahneman, Daniel. *Thinking, Fast and Slow.* New York: Farrar, Straus and Giroux, 2011. – Provides foundational insights on cognitive biases and heuristics.

3. Tetlock, Philip E., and Dan Gardner. *Superforecasting: The Art and Science of Prediction.* New York: Crown, 2015. – Demonstrates how disciplined probabilistic thinking improves forecasting accuracy.

Randomness, Risk, and Uncertainty

1. Gigerenzer, Gerd. *Risk Savvy.* New York: Penguin, 2014. – Explores practical approaches to understanding risk and probability.

2. Taleb, Nassim Nicholas. *The Black Swan.* New York: Random House, 2007. – Introduces the concept of rare, high-impact events ("Black Swans") and their effect on systems.

3. Knight, Frank H. *Risk, Uncertainty, and Profit.* Boston: Houghton Mifflin, 1921. – Classic work distinguishing measurable risk from true uncertainty.

Cognitive Biases and Mental Models

1. Munger, Charlie. *Poor Charlie's Almanack.* Charlottesville: Donning Company, 2005. – Discusses mental models and multidisciplinary thinking for decision-making.

2. Bevelin, Peter. *Seeking Wisdom.* CreateSpace, 2009. – Provides practical applications of mental models and cognitive frameworks.

3. Parrish, Shane. *The Great Mental Models* series. Farnam Street Publishing, 2019–present. – Guides on applying mental models across multiple domains.

Investing, Entrepreneurship, and Optionality

1. Thiel, Peter. *Zero to One.* New York: Crown Business, 2014. – Insights on creating high-value, asymmetric opportunities.

2. Ries, Eric. *The Lean Startup.* New York: Crown Business, 2011. – Introduces iterative experimentation and minimum viable products.

3. Taleb, Nassim Nicholas. *Antifragile.* New York: Random House, 2012. – Explores systems that benefit from volatility, stress, and uncertainty.

Decision-Making, Scenario Planning, and Resilience

1. Hammond, John S., Ralph L. Keeney, and Howard Raiffa. *Smart Choices: A Practical Guide to Making Better Decisions.* Boston: Harvard Business Review Press, 1999.

2. Kahneman, Daniel, and Amos Tversky. "Prospect Theory: An Analysis of Decision under Risk." *Econometrica,* 1979. – Foundational paper on behavioral economics and loss aversion.

3. Lindley, Dennis. *Making Decisions.* New York: Wiley, 1985. – Introduces Bayesian updating and decision theory applications.

General References and Further Reading

1. Farnam Street Blog (www.farnamstreetblog.com) – Articles and resources on mental models, decision-making, and probabilistic thinking.

2. Khan Academy: Probability & Statistics – Free online courses for building foundational probabilistic knowledge.

3. Coursera and edX – Online courses on decision science, risk management, and cognitive frameworks.

4. National Bureau of Economic Research (www.nber.org) – Working papers on finance, risk, and strategic decision-making.

Note: The above references provide a foundation for understanding probabilistic thinking, decision-making under uncertainty, and cognitive tools for high-quality choices. Readers are encouraged to explore these works for deeper insights, practical exercises, and advanced frameworks.

9 789334 458992

Printed at Repro India Ltd.